Sail Away Ladies

Stories of Cape Cod Women in the Age of Sail

Sail Away Ladies

Stories of Cape Cod Women in the Age of Sail

JIM COOGAN

Harvest Home Books
East Dennis, Massachusetts

Sail Away Ladies

Sail away ladies, Sail away far.
Chart your course across the waves.
and mark your passage by a star.

Sail away ladies, Sail on free.
Daughters of the rolling deep,
your bridal bed is on the sea.

Sail away ladies, navigate the foam.
Whales and tales and howling gales,
now find you far from home.

Sail away ladies, knock on Neptune's door.
And with your Captain close beside,
stand against the ocean's roar.

By the Author

Mary Matthews Bray boards her father's clipper ship, National Eagle. *Painted by Caroline Ellis of Yarmouthport*

For all the ladies in my life – especially Beth.

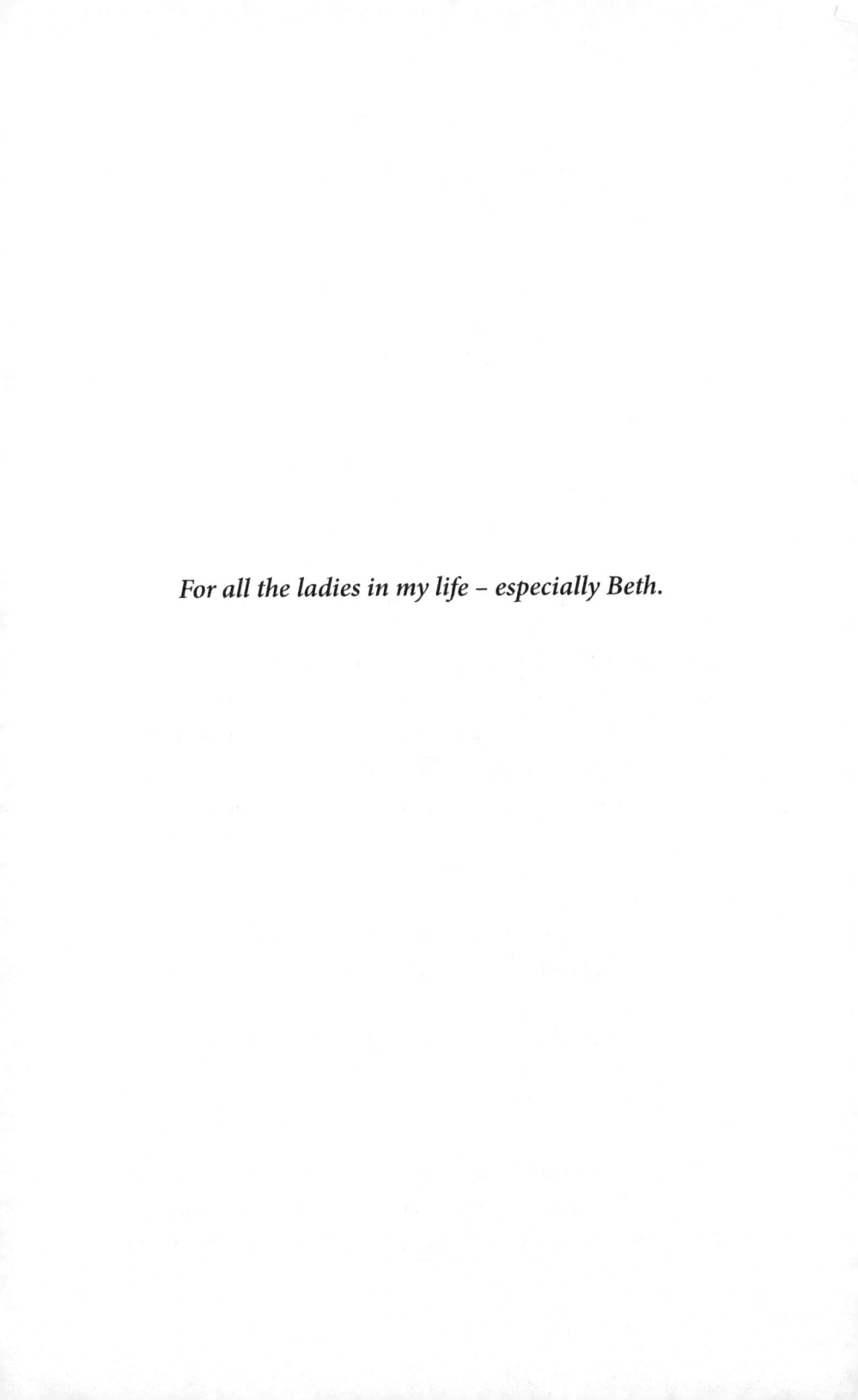

Sail Away Ladies

First Printing – October 2003
Second Printing – July 2005
Third Printing – June 2008
Fourth Printing – February 2012
Fifth Printing – January 2017
Sixth Printing – October 2023

Published by
Harvest Home Books
PO Box 1181
East Dennis, MA 02641

Copyright © 2003 by Jim Coogan

No part of this book may be reprinted or reproduced in any form without written permission from the author, except for brief passages quoted as part of a review in a newspaper or magazine. For information, contact Harvest Home Books at the address above.

ISBN 0-9672596-4-9

Cover design and text layout by
Rockwell Design, West Yarmouth, MA.

Printed in the United States of America

ISBN 0-9672596-4-9

For additional copies of Sail Away Ladies, or to inquire about the author's previous Cape Cod-related books, please write to Harvest Home Books at the address above.

Contents

	Introduction	11
I.	Experiences of Life at Sea	19
II.	Mary Chipman Lawrence of Falmouth	49
III.	Ulah Harding Reed of Chatham	69
IV.	Persis Crowell Addy of Dennis	73
V.	Lucy Lord Howes of Dennis	79
VI.	Rebecca Wood Howes of South Yarmouth	87
VII.	Clara Cook Ryder of Provincetown	101
VIII.	Viola Fish Cook of Provincetown	119
IX.	Didama Kelley Doane of West Harwich	131
X.	Bethia Knowles Mayo Sears of Brewster	145
XI.	Clara Freeman of Brewster	145
XII.	Sarah Priscilla Weekes of Harwich	155
XIII.	Sally Mayo Dyer Lavender of Provincetown	167
	Acknowledgments	187
	Notes	191
	Bibliography	201
	About the Author	207

Classification of Ships

Ship
3 or 4 masts
square rigged

Schooner
2 or more masts
fore-and-aft rigged

Bark
3 masts
2 square rigged
1 fore-and-aft rigged

Barkentine
3 masts
1 square rigged
2 fore-and-aft rigged

Brig
2 masts
both square rigged

Hermaphrodite Brig
2 masts
1 square rigged
2 fore-and-aft rigged

INTRODUCTION

I have written and lectured on the subject of Cape Cod history for almost thirty years. During this time, while researching a variety of topics related to the Cape, probably not surprisingly, I have been drawn to numerous references about the sea and its influence on the development of Barnstable County. I grew up in Brewster, Massachusetts, and no doubt, absorbed much of the sea lore of the town as a youngster. Brewster, after all, is known as "the sea captain town."

The maritime history of the Cape has always emphasized the exploits and adventures of these so-called "Blue Water Men." These were the legendary captains who drove great ships through all of the navigable waters of the globe, burnishing the reputation of Cape Cod in every world port. Many books have been written about these mariners and it is mainly through their eyes that we have formed our impressions of the nature of life at sea. Theirs was a male-oriented world of adventure, fortune, and occasionally, misfortune in the land of Neptune's empire. For centuries the sea called Cape Codders to its shifting and often untrustworthy environment, rewarding some handsomely, occasionally taking the lives and fortunes of others who were not so lucky, and ultimately, affecting all who entered its realm.

That this was a world closed to women seemed to me initially, almost a given. There were no books about them nor were there any major references to women ever being at sea. Nineteenth century writers, including Herman Melville and Richard Henry Dana, created male-centered adventures of life at sea. Indeed, traditional superstitions held that women aboard ships were unlucky for vessel and crew and it was expected that proper ladies, at least, would maintain their associations with sailors from afar. No doubt, I accepted this as fact.

Yet the truth is that there were hundreds, probably thousands of women who participated in sea adventures in those earlier days. Only recently has their story become known. Perhaps it was because few historians expected to find women involved in long sailing voyages that meaningful research into their experiences has been so late to surface. Maybe it was because men generally have done most of the history writing. It could also be that the presence of women at sea was common enough that contemporary writers failed to see it as unique and thus never focused much attention on it.

More recent scholarship has fortunately recognized the importance of the feminine presence and perspective of sea voyaging and a number of wonderful books have emerged that shed light on this heretofore overlooked area of maritime history. That Cape Cod would have had its own fair share of women making sea voyages would seem only natural given the geography of the peninsula and sea oriented culture. Many sea captains from Cape Cod took their wives with them as they traveled the sea lanes of the world. The practice was actually far more common than once assumed.

Indeed, there was a strong attitude in the nineteenth century that it was a wife's duty to accompany her husband at sea. We can get a sense of that in one of the letters sent by Anna Eldridge Hallet to her husband Captain Bangs Hallet of Yarmouthport. Anna had found her experiences at sea to be anything but pleasant. She was constantly sick and in 1859 when her husband left on a voyage to Asia, she did not accompany him. There is a measure of guilt reflected in one of her notes to him. "Bangs, if you don't blame me how glad I shall be but don't say you don't if you do. Tell me the worst of your feelings. I know I don't feel that well at sea but I should have come without giving that much thought... I have never felt anyything like it in my life to think that I could not comply with your oft repeated wishes, and orders to come."[1]

Many other pieces of correspondence show clearly that she believed that she had "hurt his feelings" by absenting herself from the voyage. Fortunately, Bangs Hallet was an understanding husband and very much in love with his wife. His replies to Anna show his concern for her feelings and his acceptance that she could not be by his side.

In many cases, however, captains demanded that their wives accompany them on sea voyages as part of an almost unwritten corollary to the marriage contract. If the women were reluctant to go aboard, they were usually wise enough to mask their feelings with journal references about the importance of "ties of affection." A few, like Sylvia Snow Taylor Park of West Harwich, penned the feelings of many wives in a Christmas letter to her children while aboard her husband's bark, the *Acme*, as the ship hammered its way around the stormy Cape Horn. "A sailor's wife a sailor's star shall be; so to be that star, I must shine forth, and let not the saddened, heartsickering [sic.] that oppresses my being, show forth."[2]

Many women actually did find the sea experience exhilarating and enjoyable. Emily Crosby Lincoln of Brewster sailed for years with her husband Joseph aboard his bark *Mist* and her surviving letters indicate that she was well satisfied with the seagoing life. Others like Sally Mayo Lavender of Provincetown found it a miserable and most uncomfortable experience. In an 1854 four-month voyage to the Mediterranean and back aboard the brig *Panama*, she made constant reference to her discomfort and llloneliness. She candidly cited other things, like the "bowel complaint," leaving little doubt that she would have much more preferred her "husband's society" if it might only have been shared on dry land.

Unlike their sisters who stayed at home, seagoing women were very much a part of the traditional rhythms and patterns of the seagoing life. For captains who liked order at sea as well as in their homes, having a wife aboard was a definite asset. Seafaring women were exposed to and were part of an environment that challenged them mentally and physically. They experienced storms, shipwrecks, the threat of pirates, exotic cultures, questionable food, childbirth at sea, and constant bouts with seasickness. "Paying old Neptune," as *mal de mer* was referred to, new no gender barriers. These women played nursemaid to their own children and occasionally acted as surrogate mothers to some of the younger crewmen. As missionaries, nurses, and helpmates to their husbands, seagoing women had access to a very different world than did their female relatives who remained ashore. The journals and letters written by these ladies provide historians with a valuable reflection on what life was really like aboard sailing vessels and a perspective that was very different from that offered by sailors who took the time to record their own feelings about life on the deep.

Women's sea journals fall into four general categories. The first is the Travel Diary, which was an open record of the ship's itinerary. Essentially, this was a daily recording of things of interest that would later be shared with people at home. Similar in nature was the Public Journal. Like the Travel Diary, the Public Journal set down shipboard events that the writer wanted to tell her relatives and friends. Two others, the Journal of Conscience and the Daily

This picture of Anna Hallet was painted in Canton, China. It was not done from life because women were not allowed into Canton at the time. Captain Hallet probably described his wife to the artist or may have provided a sketch to work from. Picture courtesy of the Historical Society of Old Yarmouth.

Record, were more personal in nature. These served as a sort of reflective philosophical account of the inner feelings and emotions of the woman who made the entries. They were often very personal and were noot usually written for others to read. Often, they would be destroyed by the writer upon the completion of the voyage. The examples that survive, perhaps unconsciously overlooked in long packed away trunks, are the most revealing in terms of true feelings and as such, they provide historians with summations of the real thoughts and emotions of the women who kept them.

Journal keeping in this period was also viewed by some as a necessary discipline and while most women took up the task willingly, there were some who found it a chore rather than a positive experience. But even in these, the detail of life at sea was far more descriptive than the chronicles of most sailors. Men's journals and logbooks were often perfunctory accounts concerning concrete events and notations concerning wind, weather, and ship positions. They were not usually moved to make note of personal situations. Captain Thomas Lawrence of Falmouth, for example, while master of the whaling bark *Alto*, neglected to mention the birth of his daughter Amelia in the Azores, but he did remember to enter the barometer reading in his logbook on that same date.

Thirty years ago it was quite a shock for me to find that, first of all, women had ever been present aboard sailing ships, and second, that there had been so many of them. Subsequently, in coming across an increasing number of references to seagoing women from Cape Cod, I became interested in their experiences in an environment that was for that time, certainly and very decidedly a male domain. As I have always believed that history in general should include the stories of all of the participants, so also do I feel that the story of women at sea needs to be told and celebrated. The accounts and stories of the women in this book will hopefully proof the women in this book will hopefully prove useful in broadening our view of maritime history and, by making the historical record more inclusive, serve to better reflect what that experience truly was.

• • •

Chapter 1

*"One Would Think I Intended
To Be Gone A Dozen Years"*

Experiences of Life at Sea

It is difficult to pin down when the first Cape Cod woman made a sea voyage. Certainly it is very possible that as early as the mid-seventeenth century women were making trips aboard coasting vessels. As the Plymouth colony extended its trade routes north to the settlements in Boston Bay, traveling by ship became a common necessity, most likely involving men and women.

The eighteenth century saw an extension of trade patterns into the Gulf of Maine and also to ports along the Connecticut and Long Island shore. While there is scarce documentation concerning these unscheduled voyages, we can make a safe assumption that women occasionally traveled aboard ships bound for these places. Most of these trips would have lasted days rather than weeks and could not be considered much of a departure from life ashore because of their short duration. Women went on these abbreviated sea excursions if they had a need to connect with an outside market and they usually traveled with other women as companions.

It was the nineteenth century that saw the first extended

sea voyages involving women from the Cape and Islands. The industry that brought about this change was whaling. Cape Codders had always chased whales, learning the craft from the indigenous natives shortly after settlement. In fact, it was a Cape Cod man from Yarmouth, Ichabod Paddock, who traveled to Nantucket in 1690 to teach the islanders the trade. The catching of whales offshore commenced with this period and flourished through the eighteenth century. Unlike the century that followed, however, whaling in the 1700's did not usually involve long voyages. Sailors might be away from port for perhaps as much as a month hunting whales. This was not much different from the thousands of small fishing vessels that worked the offshore Grand Banks harvesting mackerel, cod, and haddock. Women played no role aboard these ships.

But as the nineteenth century search for whales took ships and crews further and further from the Cape and Islands, and as voyages turned into months and years, the custom of bringing the wives of whaling masters aboard began. Nantucket's Mary Russell was perhaps one of the first to make an extended sea voyage, leaving Nantucket in 1817 aboard the whaler *Hydra* and not returning to her home for almost three years. Her experience opened the doors to other women who began to see life aboard ship as a more common practice. Within just a few years of Mary Russell's voyage, literally hundreds of women from the Cape and Islands were accompanying their sea captain husbands on world voyages lasting anywhere from three to five years.

A missionary in Hawaii, Reverend Samuel C. Damon noted the change in 1858, citing over forty whalers in the Pacific with women aboard and commented on their "goodly influence.'" By the mid-nineteenth century, it was hard to find a seacoast town from Long Island to the coast of Maine that did not boast a fair number of women who had experienced life aboard ship. One estimate has it that by 1850 one in four sea captains was accompanied aboard by his wife.

Far from being proto-feminists, the women who went to sea with their husbands were actually attempting to preserve a traditional marriage role. Women who stayed home to run farms and manage businesses were far more progressive and independent. Seagoing women did not see themselves as breaking any new ground socially. With longer voyages, many women in seacoast towns could point to marriages without men. The male population of many Cape Cod towns was divided into those who were away on voyages, those who were returning from one, and those who were preparing to start one. Fairly typical were the circumstances of Harriet Gifford of Falmouth who had lived with her husband Captain Henry Gifford only ten months out of the first five years of their marriage. Going to sea with their husbands was not so much a political statement for these women as it was an understandable urge to hold a family unit together against otherwise long separations.

Clara Cook Ryder of Provincetown was typical of this new breed of seagoing women. Married in 1851 to whaler Stephen A. Ryder, she was aboard his 241-ton bark *N.D. Chase* in 1857 when the vessel made a twenty-seven month voyage into the Indian Ocean. At age twenty-six, this was her first sea voyage and she had her two sons with her, Elijah who was five years old, and her baby, Frank who was two. During the trip, the *N.D. Chase* visited the Azores and chased whales along the west African coast before heading south around the Cape of Good Hope in a cruise that subjected Clara to violent storms, near mutiny, sea sickness, and the birth of a son at sea with her husband assisting in the delivery. It was nothing like home. In her journal she expressed frustration at her inability to keep her boys and her husband clean during the dirty business of "cutting in" a whale. But she was realistic about what a successful whale hunt meant. "I sewed and knit some but everything is so black and dirty that I cannot

The excitement of a seagoing adventure was always tempered by the sense of separation from those remaining at home. The Century Magazine, August 1890. Courtesy of Cape Cod Community College.

do much but wash the children for they are a blue black most of the time. But I do not mind the dirt if we can only get the oil."[1]

Clara Ryder's experiences aboard a whaler paralleled those of fellow "sister sailor" Georgianna Johnston Dyer who was also from the Cape tip. Shortly after their marriage in April of 1893, she accompanied her husband, Captain Joseph Emmons Dyer, aboard the 130-ton schooner *Ellen A. Swift* to the Atlantic whaling grounds. It was the first of five voyages with her husband that would span ten years. Much later, when recalling her days at sea, Mrs. Dyer indicated that the routine was anything but romantic. She remembered shipboard life as tedious and monotonous, with little time to break the boredom. On going to sea she said, "I used to say to the cook, 'Cook, when I get back to Provincetown I'll walk to the end of town; they'll be such a big cloud of dust you won't be able to see me!'... I want to see all I can of land. I've had enough of water."[2]

Undoubtedly her feelings were shaped in part by rough weather and the constant threat that the *Ellen A. Swift* might founder in stormy seas. "No one can describe a hurricane right," she recalled. "It's too terrible for words. The blow hit us and we all went to the floor. There we lay, bracing our feet and catching hold of anything to keep from rolling around like balls." During one storm, Captain Dyer came below to see how his wife was handling the weather. "Are you frightened?" he asked. She replied, "Is my hair white?" He said, "No." "Well," she looked up at him. "No one's hair will ever turn white from fear."[3]

The nineteenth century also brought the first regular scheduled transatlantic commercial voyages. This fact, coupled with the growing interest in the so-called China trade, encouraged enterprising and resourceful shipmasters to become world travelers in the pursuit of maritime fortunes. Merchant ship travel had the advantage of a set destination and a cruise completion date – two aspects that were not part of whaling voyages. But women who embarked aboard merchantmen faced many of the same challenges that their whaling sisters did. Storms at sea were just as violent and there was always the possibility of being shipwrecked on an uncharted island far from the regular shipping lanes. The experience of Persis Crowell Addy of East Dennis was typical of the hazards that befell many of Cape Cod's seagoing women.

The daughter of East Dennis clipper ship owner and master mariner Captain Prince Crowell, Persis married Captain John H. Addy, a well respected deep water skipper who had recently taken up residence in the village. In 1866, in what was a honeymoon trip for the couple, they left the East Coast with a load of coal and merchandise aboard the 648-ton Dennis-built clipper *Christopher Hall*. The letter that she sent her parents from New York just before leaving turned out to be something of an understatement. "One would think," she wrote. "That I intended to be gone a dozen years or so by the fuss I make about it." Months later, while cruising in the Pacific Ocean, the *Christopher Hall* struck an uncharted reef near Apia, the capital of Western Samoa. Leaving the sinking vessel with only the clothes on her back, Persis was lowered by a rope around her waist into a small boat, which made it through the surf to a small island inhabited only by a few natives. It was a month before the survivors were able to get off.[4]

Captain Taylor Howes Jr. of Yarmouth, the skipper of the ship *John Tucker*, ran aground on an uncharted East Indies reef in 1875. Aboard the ship with him were his wife, daughter Carrie, and a baby son. They were adrift in an open boat for a week before making a landfall on the China coast. From there, with the assistance of the U.S. consul, the family traveled overland to India where they eventually secured passage for home.[5]

Mary Connolly of Dennis was aboard the ship *South America* when it began to sink off the coast of West Africa. She was lashed to the mizzenmast by her husband, Captain James Connolly, and later, as the ship settled, to the deck rail. After a night of fear,

Sickness took Bourne's Amelda Tobey's life far from home. Photo by Jim Coogan.

Experiences of Life at Sea

A Brewster woman, Susan Lincoln, was lost at sea. Photo by Jim Coogan.

the crew was able to build a raft from pieces of wreckage and the survivors floated to shore. Before they were rescued, Mrs. Connolly experienced near starvation and the constant menace of hostile native tribes. The ordeal quite probably led to her delivery of a stillborn child shortly after her return home. Still worse was the fate of Susan Paine Lincoln, the wife of Brewster Captain Joseph Lincoln, who was swept overboard in a storm off the Virginia Capes. She was just one of many women who never returned home to Cape Cod from a sailing voyage.

When the *Mary S. Ames* was shipwrecked in a hurricane off the coast of Madagascar in June of 1894, Captain Samuel F. Knowles of Orleans had his pregnant wife Amber and their three-year old daughter Louisa with him. After several days in a small boat, the survivors reached land. The presence of the white child is probably what saved the survivors. It seems that the coastal natives, who were reputed to be cannibals, were fascinated with the little girl. They considered Louisa to be an angel who had been cast ashore for them to worship. Alerted to their presence by the natives, French authorities arrived at the hut where the Captain and his family had been detained and rescued them. The survivors were brought overland to the port of Tamatave where they were eventually able to gain passage back to the United States.[6]

During rough weather in the Gulf of Mexico aboard the barkentine *Henry Norwell*, the wife of Captain Jarius Allen of Harwichport was encouraged to leave the badly leaking vessel for the safety of a passing streamer. Despite her husband's urging, she stayed aboard and lent a hand to keeping the ship afloat. "I spent most of my time making hot tea for him, and lemonade for the others," she recalled. "When there wasn' anything else to do, I sat and embroidered." Her steadiness in the face of danger apparently made a strong impression on the crew. When the terrified cook saw Mrs. Allen calmly sitting in her cabin embroidering a linen table cloth, he said, "Well, ma'am, if you can do that, I guess we aren't going to sink right off. I might as well go make the boys a pie."[7]

Even a voyage in local waters could be fraught with danger. In January of 1881, when Captain William Crowell of West Dennis took his wife Abbie aboard his schooner, the *Uriah B. Fisk*, bound for Charleston, South Carolina, they encountered gale winds and heavy drift ice off Monomoy Island. Unable to get an anchor to hold, the schooner went aground at Great Point, Nantucket and after sixteen hours of pounding began to break up. Fortunately, the lighthouse keeper there raised the alarm and a rescue team was assembled from Siasconset village. Leaping ice cake to ice cake, the rescuers made it out to the stranded hulk, eventually getting everyone safely ashore.

"But I S'pose The Old Lady Would Feel Bad."

Rough crews could be just as much a problem as rough weather. When Mary Matthews Bray of Yarmouth got her first look at the sailors coming aboard her father's ship *National Eagle*, she was quite shocked. "Most of them were intoxicated," she wrote. "They staggered over the side of the ship, bringing with them their few possessions. Some of them apparently had nothing but the clothes they stood in; others brought small bundles; a few had canvas bags of varying sizes. They were hoisted on board like bales of merchandise, and were then roughly taken up and carried to their quarters in the forecastle. It was a discouraging spectacle."[8]

The recruitment of sailors for long voyages was never an easy task and the quality of those who ended up manning ships was often not the best. In the months before a voyage, a captain would contract with a shipping office for a certain number of men. When they came aboard, he rarely knew their backgrounds or their reasons for going to sea. This was particularly true of whaling ships where foremast hands often had to literally be "shanghaied" for the three and four-year voyages. It was common to employ "crimpers," who were unscrupulous recruiters that

Advertisements such as this one in the Whaleman's Shipping List, and Merchants' Transcript, ancouraged young men to seek employment at sea.

Experiences of Life at Sea

would promise just about anything to lure sailors into a contract that might barely make expenses over a four-year voyage.

Consequently, crews were often rebellious and difficult to manage. The presence of a woman on a ship could and did, however, sometimes serve as a restraint on the actions of a captain in the disciplining of his crew. At the very least, "lady sailors" made life in the aft cabin and on the quarter deck more cheerful. Many sailors knew and appreciated the fact that punishment for shipboard infractions was usually not as severe when the captain's wife was aboard. One crewmember acknowledged this in saying, "I'd as soon kill the captain as I would a kitten. But I s'pose the old lady would feel bad."[9] This may have been one case where the captain's wife, by simply being aboard, prevented a mutiny.

A Yarmouth girl, Ida Belle Taylor, actually did help her sea captain father put down a mutiny aboard his ship the *A.M. Lawrence*. In 1860, while anchored in a South American port, some members of the crew moved to take over the ship. They grabbed Captain Gorham Taylor Jr., striking him and knocking him almost senseless to the deck. Six-year old Ida Bell went below to his cabin and brought up two loaded pistols concealed in her skirt. She slipped her father the pistols. Recovering from the blow, the captain was able to grab one of the ring leaders of the mutiny and, holding the pistol to the rebellious sailor's head, he forced the others to abandon their plan and surrender.[10] Another woman, Mary Gorham Baker, wife of Captain Ezekiel Baker of Hyannis, used her own method of putting a quick end to a mutiny aboard the clipper ship *Young America*. When workers, unloading the ship off Colon, Panama, threatened to take over, Mrs. Baker hoisted the mutiny flag from her cabin window, catching the attention of the American naval vessel *U.S.S. Tennessee*, which was anchored nearby. The *Young America* was boarded by Marines who put the mutineers in irons.[11]

The security of many foreign ports often left much to be

desired and the possibility that robbers might attempt to board vessels at anchor was always a worry. In May of 1886, while in the harbor at Rio De Janeiro, the barkentine *Rebecca Crowell* was boarded by robbers who were able to make their way into the captain's darkened cabin. Esther Kelley Crowell, the wife of Captain Luther Crowell of West Dennis, was sleeping with her little girl, and was awakened by the sound of the intruders. She roused her husband with a shout that someone was in the room. He jumped out of his bed and fired a pistol at the nearest dark shape, causing the robbers to drop everything and flee the ship. As the robbers swam for shore, Captain Crowell hastened their departure with a few following pistol shots. Despite the fact that they had frustrated the robbery, Mrs. Crowell wrote to her sister that she spent a number of subsequent sleepless nights in fear that the robbers might return and this time kill her out of anger at having their thievery thwarted.[12]

"They Behaved Themselves Like Men."
So wrote Clara Cook Ryder in reference to the behavior of her two small sons after an Atlantic storm battered the whaler *N.D. Chase*. The children of sea captains often spent many of their early years getting an education aboard ship before they ever attended regular schools on land. Raising and caring for little ones at sea was something that many Cape Cod women accepted as being a natural consequence of accompanying their husbands aboard ship. The sea was a unique and dangerous environment, requiring perhaps a good deal more parental supervision than would have been the case in raising children at home.

Watching out that children didn't get hurt while climbing in the ship's rigging, or making sure that stormy weather didn't wash them overboard was one of the responsibilities of families with children aboard ship. Esther Crowell noted in one of her letters to her friend Annie Doane that her little daughter Grace

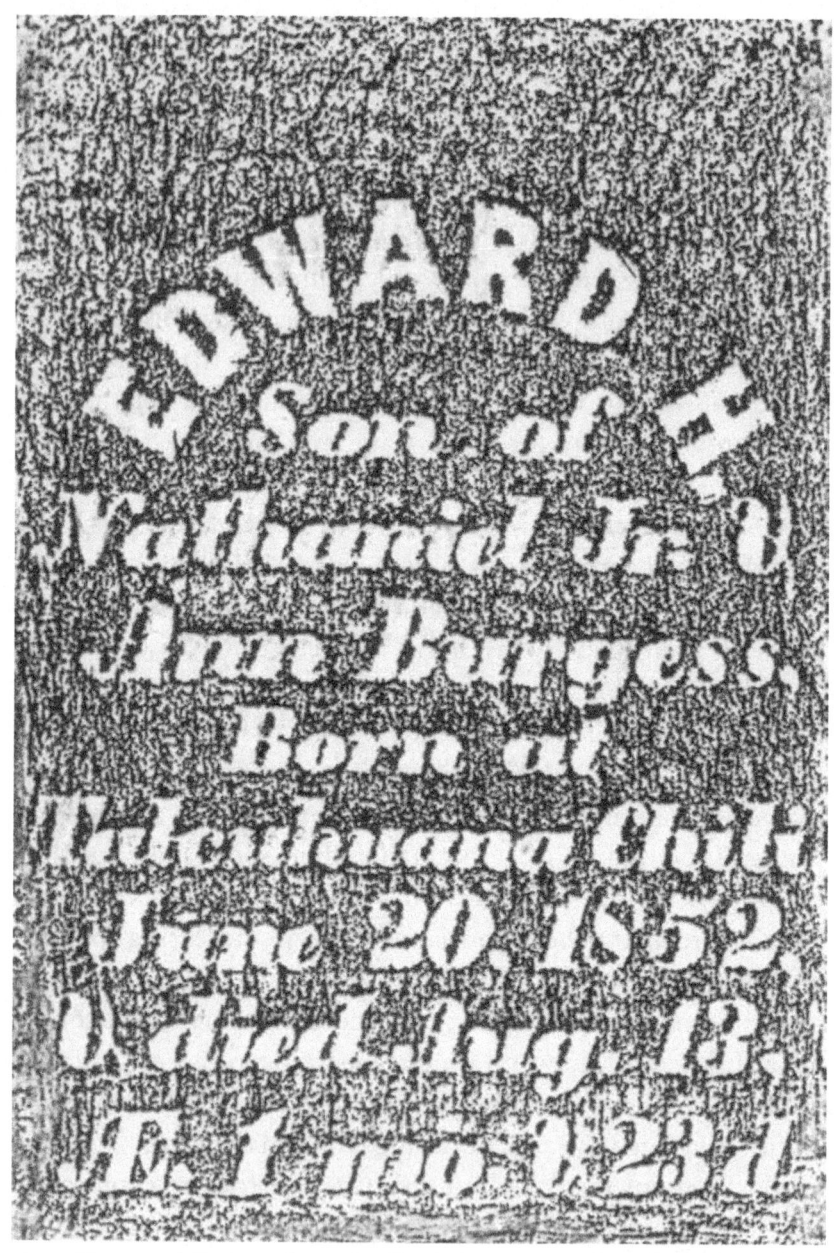

Ann Cammett Burgess brought her infant son, Edward, back to Cape Cod in a liquor cask to rest in ground he never saw in life.

was upended in rough seas while sitting in her high chair. "...the vessel gave a terrible lurch. I saw the high chair tip and I threw myself forward to try and save her from going over. I couldn't quite reach her in time. The chair went over and she fell with a crash on the floor, her head just missing the edge of the table. I got to Grace and picked her up, finding her bruised and frightened but not badly hurt."[13]

Even the presumed safety of a port was no guarantee that children would be out of harm's way. On a voyage to Portugal, Blanche Howes, daughter of Captain Marcus Howes of Dennis, was kidnapped by people who were intrigued with the color of the child's blond hair. Fortunately, she was rescued by her father before any serious harm could come to her.

But some children were not so lucky. In 1852, Ann Cammett Burgess, wife of Captain Nathaniel Burgess of Monument Beach, lost her two-month old baby boy, Edward, to sickness in Chile while aboard the whaler *Robert Edwards*. Because the child had not yet been baptized, he could not be buried there. Mrs. Burgess had the infant's body placed in a liquor cask and brought home to Bourne where he was buried in the Monument Beach cemetery on County Road.[14] Losing a child overboard was always a worry. In March of 1856, while on board the 197-ton bark *Turk*, little Elisha Harding Jr. of Chatham escaped the grasp of his mother Julia's hand and fell off the after deck house into the sea. "It was not but a second I started to go to him," she wrote in a letter home. "I looked on the house, he was gone. I looked in the water to see my child on his back with his little face and hands just above the water." Despite a search in the gathering darkness, the little boy was never found.[15]

Tutors were often kept aboard to see that children did not fall behind in their studies. Musical instruments, which included pianos and organs, were occasionally part of the seagoing curriculum. Without doubt, perhaps the most closely studied subject was geography as youngsters plotted their positions while the ship made its way along the trade routes. Clara Augusta Ellis of West Harwich, the only daughter of Captain Thomas Ellis, had seen six continents before she was eighteen years old. She would tell her grandchildren that, as a young woman, she had known Amsterdam, Liverpool, Canton, Hong Kong, and other foreign ports better than she knew the villages of Cape Cod.[16] Bertha Hamblin Boyce of West Falmouth got a chance to meet "the Chief of Madagascar" while cruising the Indian Ocean aboard her father's whaleship *Islander*. "He had seven wives," she recalled in a memoir written years later. ". . . They were dark skinned of course, being Africans, and they were dressed in white. Their lips were blood red from chewing betel nuts. I tell the girls that is where they got the idea of using lipstick."[17]

Pets were exotic playthings for these youngsters. In addition to the barnyard animals that were housed on deck for food, monkeys, tropical birds, and dogs made up the types of animals that were found aboard ships. Kittens and goats also learned to accommodate the roll of the ship as companions for seagoing children. Esther Crowell thought it amusing that her son Bertie kept his pet cockroaches in little matchboxes in the aft cabin.[18] "We had many pets," wrote Kate Baker Chase of Harwich, remembering her trip as a five-year old with her father aboard the wheat clipper *Sterling*. "Cats, kittens, puppies, rabbits, and a little kid with its mother that gave milk to us children, which I detested because I was made to drink it warm. The last pets given me were two bantams, given by the port doctor in Rangoon. Queer little things, their curly feathers curled toward their heads. 'Mrs. Pedley,' named for the doctor, laid one egg, then quit."[19] One of the more unusual cases of a child having a pet aboard a ship was when Louisa Marie Sears prevailed upon her father, Captain Joshua Sears of East Dennis and master of the clipper ship *Wild Hunter*, to allow her to bring her pet pony aboard the

Louisa "Lulu" Sears prevailed upon her father to let her ride her pony on the Wild Hunter. *Courtesy of Mrs. Frank Eastman.*

vessel. A seagoing stall was built and each day little "Lulu" would exercise her animal by riding him around the main deck.[20]

One story told by old timers in Barnstable was about a little girl named Daisy whose father, a Captain Percival, was a Mediterranean fruit trader. On one voyage Daisy was given a canary in Sicily. It became very tame and flew around the deck quite happily. When the ship arrived in Philadelphia to unload cargo, the bird flew away into the city much to the consternation of the child. After three days they sailed for New York. Just before nightfall, as they entered the crowded harbor near Staten Island, out of the sky came the canary to join them on their trip back to Cape Cod.

Children born at sea often carried that fact with them for the rest of their lives in the names that they were given. A typical middle name of a child who first entered the world aboard a ship might be "Seaborn," or "Woodhull." Often the actual

Foreign parts like Canton, China were familiar places to seagoing women from Cape Cod. In places like this, women would be expected to entertain other captains and their families. Picture courtesy of the Historical Society of Old Yarmouth.

location of the birth would be reflected as well. When Caroline Nye Sherman of Sandwich gave birth to a daughter at Herschel Island in the high latitudes of the Arctic, the child was given the name Helen "Herschel" Sherman. Names like Annie "Malacca" Nickerson and Celia "De Verde" Crowell forever marked these children with the places of their birth. Elizabeth Baxter, the wife of Captain Benjamin D. Baxter of Hyannis, had her daughter Annie born aboard the Burma bound ship *John N. Cushing* in 1873. Combining both location and designation of birth at sea, the little girl was named Annie Malacca Seaborn Baxter. One Provincetown sea captain, while assisting in the birth of his daughter, vowed during his wife's difficult labor that if she bore him a healthy child he would name the baby after the first bird he saw when he went up on deck. As luck would have it, when he went topside, the first bird in sight was an albatross. His daughter subsequently went through life as "Trossy" Bangs.

"You Would Soon Get Used To Seeing Naked Men."
Seagoing ladies were eyewitnesses to exotic cultures and customs that were very different from what they were used to seeing on Cape Cod. They commented in their journals about the often strange and sometimes frightening practices that they observed while in and around foreign ports. Some of their observations have a contemporary ring. While visiting Marseilles, France, Sally Mayo Lavender voiced the universal shopper's woe "...we went to a number of other stores, where all you wanted was money! money! money! and with this you might obtain whatever you wished."[21] In a similar vein, Brewster's Mary Knowles wrote to her cousin from Hong Kong in September of 1867 about the Chinese merchants that she had to deal with there. "I have bought a few little things but it takes some time to learn to deal with them. They are such cheats. They ask two or three times as much for an article as they expect to get."[22]

Nineteenth-century Cape Cod women enjoyed shopping in London's West End, and visiting the many museums of European port cities. They entertained other sailing families in Hong Kong and Yokohama. They admired the Tivoli gardens in Copenhagen, climbed the Leaning Tower of Pisa, and collected shells from the beach at Kowloon. The wives and daughters of sea captains became inveterate travelers, recording their impressions, favorable and otherwise, of foreign cities from Melbourne to Buenos Aires.

Visiting new places could provoke concerns about accommodations. Clara Cook Ryder worried a bit about sleeping in her hotel at Fayal in the Azores. "...the rest of the day I spent in reading, talking, and looking after the children and retired at night at eleven o'clock, hoping that little unmerciful animal called the flea will let me have a good night's rest."[23] While traveling through a rural area of China in 1856, Bethia Bearse, wife of Captain Richard Bearse of Hyannis, was mobbed by Chinese women who attempted to lift up her dress and look at her legs. Their motive was curiosity. Many of them had been subjected to the practice of foot binding and had never seen a woman with normal sized feet![24] Hersilia Basset, wife of Zenas D. Basset who was master of the Barnstable bark *Hersilia*, so fascinated an African chieftain that he declared his intentions to buy her.[25] On a voyage to Cuba in 1875, Anna Crowell of Dennis apparently ignored a law that said that women were not allowed to walk in the city without a male escort. She did it anyway and because of her transgression she spent a day in the Havana jail until her husband, with the assistance of the American consul, was able to arrange her release.

Victorian sensitivities were very often challenged in foreign ports. While watching natives load cargo aboard her husband's ship *Mist* in Cocanada, India, Emily Crosby Lincoln wrote her sister that the scene there was much different from the same activity in Brewster. "Their dress does not cost them much for they are almost entirely naked. All the most of them wear is just a little piece of cloth and they are almost as black as the coal they are taking out of the ship. Then they wear their hair done up behind their heads in a kind of bob. They have rings in their ears, through their noses, and on their fingers and toes, also plenty of silver and brass bands around their wrists and ankles and they keep up such a chattering they are like a parcel of monkeys... I suppose you would be terribly shocked... however you would soon get used too seeing naked men."[26]

Cape Cod women were not shy in voicing their impressions of some of the foreign people and customs that they observed and it is not unusual to find a bit of "jingoistic" flavor in their comments. Emily Crosby Lincoln attributed the poverty of Leghorn, Italy to the population's support of "lazy priests."

Observing the north African coast, Sally Mayo Lavender judged the natives rather harshly. "I looked at the distant landscape as it lay stretched before me diversified with its hills and mountains presenting to the eye a green and fertile country; a country that in its appearance deserved to be inhabited by a better race than now inhabited it."[27]

"For Here Are My All!"

The typical social structure of a ship that had a woman aboard was pyramid shaped. The captain naturally occupied the apex of the pyramid, closely followed by his wife. It was very important that the woman understood clearly how much she could crowd her husband's authority. Rarely did they question their subordinate position aboard ship in their journals. Writing of her life aboard the whale ship *Addison*, Mary Chipman Lawrence saw her husband as the "prime ruler" of his own little kingdom.

If a wife appeared to play too much of a visible authoritative role, the men would lose respect for the captain and the negative expression of "Hen Frigate" would be used to describe the ship. The mates and crewmen filled in the positions toward the middle and lower end of the pyramid. The stratification was physical as well as social in that the stern section of the vessel was the exclusive domain of the captain's family. It was not expected that the crewmen would invade the family spaces in the aft cabin except for the expressed purpose of performing ship's work. Just as the men were enjoined from spending leisure time aft, so also was the wife of the captain not expected to be seen forward of the main mast, particularly in the area of the forecastle where the men were berthed. She spent most of her above deck time walking or sitting on the after deck house. Only the first mate dined regularly at the captain's table. The second and third mate, and occasionally the ship's carpenter, took their food in the captain's dining area – usually after the family had finished their meal.

If the captain's wife did not have children with her, the voyage could be especially lonely. She was in one sense privileged in rank but in another, very much deprived of the important companionship of other women. Isolated, ignored, and often ridiculed by the crew, seagoing women had only their husband's company to console them against the intense longing for home that often is reflected in their journals. This feeling seemed to manifest itself especially on Sundays when women at home would have had the society of other women while attending church services. In the nineteenth century, women attended church services on a regular basis and religion served as a focal point of their social lives. Church activity also provided a solidarity among females that gave them a respite from an otherwise hard life.

Sally Mayo Lavender, taken with melancholy one evening, wondered if anyone in Provincetown was thinking about her as her ship plowed its way across the dark ocean. "Is there anyone in the wide circle we call friends there, who has bestowed one thought on us today and thought that we were lonely, or would like us to join them in visiting the house of God?" she asked. And she justified to herself why she was at sea instead of at home. "Perhaps one might say 'You need not be there, you are not obligated to be there anymore than we.' But let me ask you which would be the worse: to be separated from the best friend I have on earth all the time for the sake of enjoying the comfort and enjoyment of the land, or share with him on the land, or share with him once in a while his privations and lonely hours? and endeavor to make them pleasanter and more cheerful? I think the latter far more preferable – though on such evenings as this, our thoughts may wander home."[28]

Part of every day was devoted to writing letters to loved ones. Correspondence was carried out by sending mail on homeward bound vessels. There were deposit points in the Pacific and Atlantic where letters could be picked up for transfer. It was

Ships meeting at sea could provide a welcome opportunity for women to have a "gam." For at least a short while, their isolation would be broken by conversation and the social interaction that women sorely lacked in their shipboard homes. Courtesy of Cape Cod Community College.

an irregular form of communication that could take weeks or months. In a few cases, letters had arrived after the writer had returned to Cape Cod – or had died at sea. With the many shipwrecks of the period, some communications never made it at all. There was no postage involved. Letters from home were addressed simply, "Mrs. Ryder, ship *N.D. Chase*, Provincetown." Sometimes the name of the captain carrying the letter would be added, e.g. "Kindness of Captain Tuck." Newspapers were eagerly shared by vessels whenever they were available.

When encountering ships at sea, vessels that had women aboard would often take the time to allow them to visit with one another. This was known as having a "gam." As both vessels maintained a steady parallel course, the woman would be slung across open water on a rope between the ships while secured in a

Hannah Rebecca Crowell Burgess, pictured with her husband, William, made a trip to China aboard the clipper ship Whirlwind *in 1854. Her Bible and wedding ring, along with some of the items that she brought back from the Far East are in front of the portraits. On a subsequent voyage aboard the clipper ship* Challenger, *when her husband became ill, Hannah navigated the ship to a port on the coast of Chile. Courtesy of the Sandwich Historical Society.*

"gamming chair," which was nothing more than a half cut barrel with a seat in it. If the sea was calm and the winds light, women could be transferred in the ship's boat. Crew members, restless in the absence of women, also looked forward to catching a glimpse of another lady in these occasions. Lewis Eldridge, aboard the New Bedford whaler *Herald* in 1867, recalled a time of "speaking" another vessel. "The captain had his wife with him and it must have been her washday for in the after rigging were hung articles of women's attire, a sight reminding all of us on the *Herald* of the clothes line at 'home, sweet home.'"[29] For the women, any break from being alone in the constant company of men was a very welcome and most anticipated occasion. But these mid-ocean visits were infrequent and always unscheduled. It could often be weeks, even months, before a woman would have a chance to have the company of another female. For the single woman aboard, the feeling of isolation must have been very intense.

The sense of loneliness and homesickness is one of the more powerful emotions that can be felt in reading a female sailing journal. Off the Azores after several weeks at sea, Sally Mayo Lavender confided her longings for her Provincetown home. "I felt sense of loneliness and homesickness is one of the more powerful emotions that can be felt in reading a female sailing journal. Off the Azores after several weeks at sea, Sally Mayo Lavender confided her longings for her Provincetown home. "I felt rather a tinge of homesickness tonight," she wrote. "But homesickness I could not call it, for this is all the home I know at present; for here are my all: husband and child."[30]

Hannah Burgess of Sandwich, sailing with her husband William aboard the clipper ship *Challenger*, occasionally let her homesickness show as she reflected on the long absence from her Sandwich home. But she made it clear where her priorities were. " I enjoy going to sea because I am with my husband. With him, any place is home. I feel, I trust, thankful that it is my happy privilege to go with him and it is my prayer to go where he goes."[31]

"Morning Spent as Usual."

For all of the time spent aboard ship, most women found the days at sea to be repetitive and without excitement. In the absence of threatening weather, life could be boring and monotonous. Few had the opportunity, as did Augusta Knowles Penniman of Eastham, who was an active and valued participant in her husband's whaling activities aboard the bark *Minerva*, to be involved in anything of great substance. For every journal entry that mentions meeting another ship, a storm, or a visit to an exciting place, there are thousands of notations about sewing, ironing, washing, and cooking – ordinary things that occupied the great majority of a woman's time. The entry by Rebecca Wood Howes aboard the clipper ship *Swallow* is typical. "September 26th, Sabbath. Fair wind tho not as much as the day or two past. Spent the most of the day in reading."[32]

The food sometimes added to the monotony of the voyage. Ships carried chickens, goats, and pigs on deck and barrels of vegetables below decks. Fresh fish was always available. But after circulating four or five basic meals each week, seagoing women longed for a bit more diversion on the dinner plate. This was especially true near the end of a long voyage. Didama Kelley Doane of West Harwich made it clear that the meals aboard the clipper ship *Rival* could have been better. "We have just been to dinner," she wrote. "Salt beef and bread and I am heartily disgusted with that and everything else today."[33]

Still, women found a number of positive things to say about being at sea. There was the excitement of seeing major world cities and their often sophisticated cultures. Unusual animals and sea creatures provided a constant source of curiosity and amusement for women unaccustomed to such things. Many women enjoyed fishing and listening to the men singing sea chanties. Accommodations aboard ship, especially in the post-Civil War period, could sometimes be better than those found at home. The main room in the aft cabin was "well fitted out" with built in sofas with some easy chairs and a good sized table. Providing overhead light was a box-like skylight with a grill of bars to protect the glass. At night, the soft glow of coal oil lamps made the cabin cozy and comfortable. In port, the family quarters would exhibit all the trappings of a typical Victorian parlor where the captain's wife was expected to entertain visiting dignitaries and the other captains who might be anchored nearby.

Kate Baker Chase of Harwich, who was aboard her father's ships from age five through age twenty-two, wrote, "Our ships were real homes. We had lovely cabins to ourselves, and everything possible for our comfort."[34] Esther Crowell described the main room in her quarters as very pretty. "I haven't a room in my house that compares with it," she wrote in a letter to her sister. "It is all paneled in dark oak and has a Brussels carpet in a very pretty pattern, on the floor. There are two windows looking out over the deck at the stern, and beneath the windows runs a long cushioned seat. Charlie (her son) loves to stand there and look out. There is a sofa at one side of the cabin and several comfortable chairs all securely fastened in their places. Against the wall opposite the windows is a large built in desk. From the ceiling hangs a swinging lamp that gives us ample light."[35]

If the ship carried a good steward, the captain's wife could expect excellent service and a more interesting menu. Hannah Burgess recognized her good fortune, noting, "We have an excellent steward. He cooks better than I can... The ship is supplied with provisions of every kind, and I am enjoying myself as well as any person who has their husband's society and everything else convenient and comfortable."[36]

At the very least, housekeeping at sea presented far fewer problems than it did for land-bound house cleaners. One woman candidly admitted that she especially liked the fact that she could just throw the trash out of the cabin window!

In even the most extraordinary of circumstances, women could find beauty at sea. As she remembered nights on the frozen deck of her husband's Arctic whaler, Viola Cook reflected on the incredible character of the winter sky. "The glories of the northern lights possess a never-ending charm as viewed from the quiet quarter deck on a calm evening with the clear cut eyes of night studding the expanse of heavens... "[37]

But even a very routine sea voyage could sometimes manage to produce an unusual experience for women who sailed with their sea captain husbands. Traveling south toward Cape Cod aboard

Despite storms and sickness, Esther Crowell of South Dennis said that she enjoyed her times at sea with her children and her husband. Courtesy of the Dennis Historical Society.

the schooner *George D. Edmands*, Edith Nickerson Coleman had enjoyed the voyage from Stonington, Maine where her husband, Captain Bennett D. Coleman had loaded stone for delivery in Connecticut. She was expecting to be dropped with her one-year old son at her home in Cotuit and the ship was within hours of making the anchorage at the "Deephole" off Dead Neck. Instead, as night fell and a heavy fog closed in near Monomoy, the captain prudently put in the anchor awaiting better visibility before attempting to pass the dangerous shoals.

The next morning, when Mrs. Coleman went up on deck, she saw over fifty other vessels anchored near them. Just then the captain called to her and told her to prepare to get off the ship. "Right here?" she asked incredulously. "Yes, right now and right here!" he replied. Captain Coleman hailed a passing clam digger in a skiff who was on his way back from Monomoy Island and hoisted his wife and child over the side to the arms of the startled shellfisherman. "Here's money for putting her up for a night in Chatham and some extra for passage on the railroad back to Barnstable in the morning." He hastily kissed Edith goodbye and as soon as the small skiff started to pull away, he got the *Edmands* underway for Connecticut. With a fair tide and a freshening breeze, Captain Coleman wanted every advantage he could get to make up for his delay and that did not include the time for even a short stop in Cotuit to deliver his wife and son home.[38]

• • •

Chapter 11

*"But Uninterrupted Happiness
Is Not For Mortals To Enjoy"*

Mary Chipman Lawrence of Falmouth

One of the most complete seagoing journals by a Cape Cod woman was kept by Mary Chipman Lawrence of West Falmouth. The account of her experiences while aboard her husband's 108-foot whaling bark *Addison* gives a picture of how a woman coped with the seemingly interminable search for the often elusive creatures that provided the basis for the fortunes of many Cape Cod shipowners. In her first, and only whaling cruise, she meticulously recorded events ranging from the mundane to the spectacular between 1856, when the ship left New Bedford, until her arrival back in the Whaling City in 1860. If a snapshot could have been taken to summarize a typical experience by a nineteenth-century whaling wife, her story would be the prototype. The source and footnote references of this summary of her voyage are from the microfilm collection of the Providence Public Library.

Samuel Lawrence, Mary's husband, came from a family of Falmouth whalers. All of his brothers, including one who died at sea, were whalers. Captain Lawrence had been to sea at an early age and had served as master of the New Bedford whaler *Lafayette*.

Mary Chapman Lawrence. Courtesy of the Falmouth Historical Society.

Under his command, that ship had been lost in 1850 after striking a reef in the Pacific. After returning home, Captain Lawrence spent several years attempting to rehabilitate his career, finally landing a position as master of the *Addison* when a previously designated captain was unable to make the sailing date on short notice. There is evidence that Samuel secured his command at least in part because of the influence of his brother, Thomas Lawrence, who owned an interest in the ship. As such, Captain Lawrence was in the position of essentially having to prove himself again when the *Addison* departed New Bedford in the late fall of 1856.

Mary Lawrence was a descendant of the prominent Chipman family of Sandwich. She was considerably younger than her husband and, at the time of the sailing, had been married nine years and was the mother of a five-year daughter, Minnie. A strongly religious woman, even by the standards of the day, she would find the cruise often an affront to her sensitivities, particularly in the actions of some of the crewmembers who exhibited a bit more earthy behavior than she would have liked. But as Thanksgiving approached in 1856, Mary Lawrence was aboard her husband's vessel because she felt that to share the traditional role of wife she needed to forsake her land-bound connections and accompany him to wherever the quest for whales might take them.

The *Addison* was a Pacific sperm whaler as opposed to the many vessels that worked the closer Atlantic whaling grounds. The ship cleared New Bedford harbor at the end of November and headed south toward the Cape Horn passage, taking just over two months to reach this often dangerous entrance to the Pacific. After initially experiencing a few days of sea sickness, Mary Lawrence settled in for the routine of life at sea. The initial fascination with the ship's daily routine soon gave way to a monotony that would be reflected in much of her journal. Despite the hopes that the ship would capture a whale en route to the Pacific, few were sighted. Off the coast of Brazil, the *Addison*'s crew were able to get a lance into

Captain Samuel Lawrence. Courtesy of the Falmouth Historical Society.

one but lost it as the huge creature sounded and headed for the deep. During that event, Mary stayed below in her cabin, unable to watch the whaleboats because she feared that she might see her husband lost. As it was, two of the boats were stove and the hunt was unsuccessful. Mary realized then that she was just an "extra" aboard a working whaleship. She seemed accepting and even grateful of that fact when she wrote, "We are supernumeraries; nothing for us to do but look on, and we avail ourselves of that privilege."[1]

Much of the time, Mary spent hours below in her cabin with her daughter Minnie. The two sewed, played, and read together. She cultivated her plants and tried to stay busy. As it was, the child was the only real companion, other than her husband, that she had. In some ways her journal became almost a reflective comrade. She was a meticulous observer and commentator and rarely missed a day without an entry. Sea animals fascinated her and she noted their different types. She became an avid fisherman but admitted that she needed help in hauling some of the larger ones aboard. Dolphin, porpoise, tuna, and even flying fish were prepared by the cook for their table. On one occasion, many of the crewmembers, including the captain and his family, became ill after eating some fried pilotfish. "Some were fortunate enough to throw them off their stomachs without any help;" she wrote. "Others were obliged to resort to emetics."[2]

Whether it was the fish or how it was prepared is open to question. The culinary skills in the galley were questionable and it was a concern for Mary. "We have a very good steward, but not as fortunate with our cooks. Are trying the fourth now (five weeks out). The first was good for nothing. The second did not like being in the galley. It made his head ache. The third had sore hands so that he could not perform duty. And I cannot say what will befall the fourth."[3]

One of Minnie's pet pigs, named "Juba," ended up as a dinner, much to the tears and sadness of the child. When the hens "Cynthia" and "Cookie" later became a chicken pie, Mary made a note to herself not to encourage the little girl to name any of the animals on board so that the child wouldn't feel so badly when they were killed. A number of vessels were sighted as the Addison made for Hawaii but only a few came close enough to exchange news and mail. Still, her entries are upbeat and optimistic during these first months at sea. "I enjoy myself here more and more every day," she wrote. "I never weary of watching old Ocean in his many varying aspects. At one time, it is as still and placid as a lake; scarcely a ripple disturbs the surface of its water. We would never dream of the treachery that lurks in his bosom. Again, the waves rise mountain-high and dash against our noble ship with re-doubled fury. Yet still we pursue our way. It is this that I enjoy most to witness... It is sublime beyond perception."[4] She grew more comfortable at sea in the first months of the new year and on February 24th she confidently noted, "I flatter myself that I have become quite a sailor." But she was apprehensive about what it would be like when the ship arrived in Hawaii. "We are about two weeks sail from the islands. I think I shall hardly know how to speak to a lady. It is now over four months since I have spoken a word to one of my own sex (except Minnie). There is one comfort at least. I have not been guilty of the sin of scandal."[5]

The island kingdom of Hawaii was reached in mid-April of 1857. Here, Mary was able to get her feet on dry land for the first time in five months and to also regain her ties with other women. The small community of Yankee whalers and missionaries at Maui gave her the opportunity to converse and relax with people who were like her. She attended church services and made friends of several of the other whaling wives who were also ashore. Some of these women would be seasonal companions over the next few years during occasional gams on the whaling grounds. Other than observing with disapproval that many of the *Addison*'s crew were behaving badly while on liberty, Mary seems to have enjoyed her short stay at Maui. She was, however, disappointed with the deportment of the natives and their customs often shocked her. Despite the efforts of the missionaries in the islands, she concluded that the islanders were a "low, degraded, and indolent set." The visit to Honolulu, where the *Addison* took two days to take on supplies, at least gave her an opportunity to take a carriage ride into the beautiful countryside. But the whales waited and on April 29th, the ship hauled her anchors and sailed north toward the Gulf of Alaska.

Pacific Arctic whaling in this pre-Civil War period was relatively new. The Gulf of Alaska and the Bering Sea had been explored by Russian seal hunters not much more than a century earlier. Alaska itself was still part of the great Russian far eastern empire. Most American whalers, if they had wives and family with them in the Pacific, preferred to leave them in Hawaii rather than subject them to the rigors of a high latitude hunt. The *Addison* was the exception. Mary Lawrence, in fact, was one of only five wives who were with their husbands in the Arctic during the 1857 season.[6]

The *Addison* cruised without success during the month of May. The sea was rough and there was a good deal of fog and rain. Although Mary and the child were not uncomfortable, she still missed the company of her friends. But she was philosophical and even a bit apologetic in revealing her desires for a wider society than the crew of the *Addison*. "How ungrateful should I be to complain." she wrote. "I also have plenty of books and an abundance of work. It would be delightful indeed to see friends near and dear, but uninterrupted happiness is not for mortals to enjoy."[7] At least there was a new cook on board. She described him as "an old man, fat, and black as ebony." But he apparently knew enough about preparing food to keep everyone happy.

It wasn't until June 6th that the ship took its first whale on this cruise, which yielded 135 barrels of oil. They took a second on June

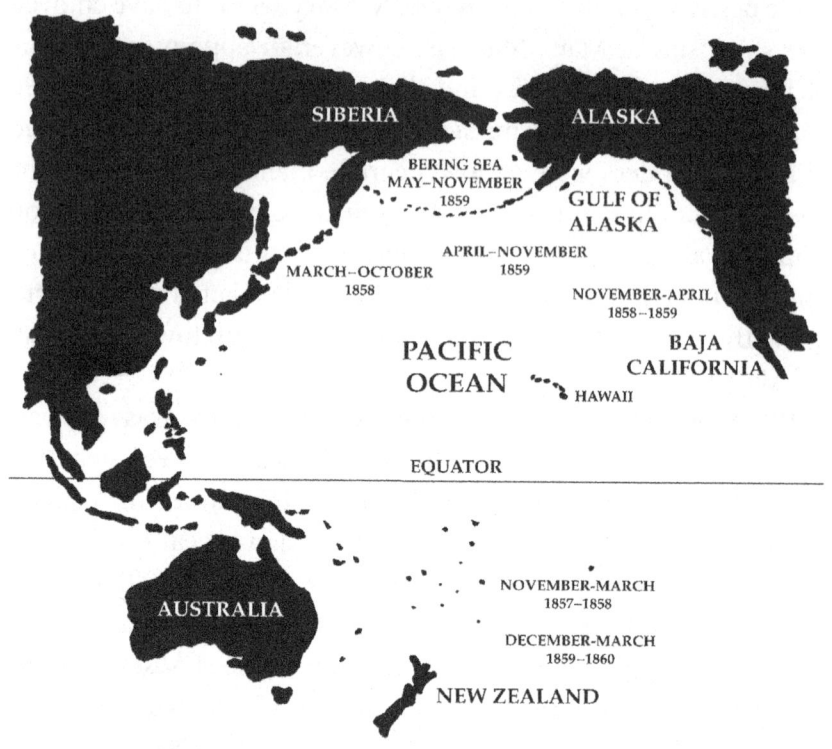

The Pacific Whaling Grounds and the cruises of the whaler Addison, *1857 through 1860.*

21st. But there was no "greasy luck" during the month of July when little Minnie celebrated her sixth birthday. The whales proved elusive and wary and, although they saw fair numbers of the creatures, by mid-September when the ship turned south for the trip back to Hawaii, they had taken only six whales and a total of about 850 barrels of oil. Much of the trip was made in bad weather and Mary and Minnie spent the majority of the cool, foggy and rainy days in their cabin. The sight of Diamond Head on October 14th was a welcome relief from the long cool Arctic summer.

Honolulu provided a chance once again to engage in social activity. Mary and her husband took a room in a small boarding house. While the captain attended to business, she was able to meet with some of the other wives that were visiting the port and she was also able to get caught up on her correspondence. The arrival of Samuel's brother, George, who was a mate on the whaler *Harvest*, was a pleasant event and she was updated on news from home. The family spent time riding in the verdant valley outside of town and visiting other ships in port. But the stop in Hawaii was only for a little less than three weeks and with November came the inevitable call to put to sea again. On November 5, 1857, the *Addison* left the islands and headed south toward the New Zealand whaling grounds.

As spring came to the southern hemisphere, the *Addison* entered the group of islands in the area northeast of New Zealand. It had been a year since they had left New Bedford and the ship had travelled over 36,000 miles. As they passed numerous volcanic islands, Mary hoped to get ashore, but the weather and heavy surf prevented her from setting foot on dry land. Some of the crew did row ashore and returned with vegetables and assorted fruits, which allowed some variation of the diet. They also captured some wild goats and hogs. Mary made pies with the gooseberries and Indian pudding from the goats' milk and bird eggs that were brought aboard.

Despite this, the Thanksgiving and Christmas holidays seemed somehow less than celebratory. Holidays were the time when home and family were most missed. Mary did her best to set a holiday table. Christmas dinner consisted of two roast turkeys, sweet and Irish potatoes, boiled onions, stewed pumpkin, and cranberries, pickles, and some of the Indian pudding that she had made. Minnie had her stocking filled with fruit and small toys. But any pleasure taken from the holiday observance was dashed when three days later the first real tragedy occurred on the cruise.

On December 28th, the cry of "Whale Ho" saw the *Addison*'s boats lowered in pursuit of a pod of finback whales. One of the boats made fast to a whale, but the angry creature lashed out with its tail and overturned the boat. An eighteen-year old Portuguese crewman named Antone was drowned. A "greenhorn," it was the young lad's first time in a whaleboat and he could not swim. The loss hit Mary particularly hard as the boy had been their cabin steward for the better part of a year. She had even discussed with her husband the possibility of adopting the boy and sending him to school when they returned to New Bedford. Mary was sick enough over the loss of the boy to take to her bed. But remorse was not something that could deter the primary mission of the ship. Later that day, more whales were spotted and the crew was able to take its first whale since leaving Hawaii.

For the better part of the next two months, the *Addison* continued to work the New Zealand whaling grounds with minimal success. Rough seas and gale force winds made any practical search for whales impossible. The crew filled a number of empty casks with salt water to provide more ballast so that the ship would ride more easily. Mary was troubled with an abscessed tooth that finally had to be lanced by her husband. In early February, the *Addison* was near Pitcairn Island but could not make a landfall because of the treacherous surf. They reached Magdalena Island in the southern Marquesas on February 9th, and anchored in the safety of the bay there. After more than three months at sea, Mary and Minnie were able to finally set foot on dry land where they were surrounded by curious natives that she described as "frightful looking creatures," and who had only previously seen one other white female on the island. There was a native missionary from Hawaii living on Magdalena. Even though she referred to him as a "Kanaka," she endorsed his efforts at Christianizing the natives. "I think it is a glorious era in the history of our world for those who once were heathen and have embraced the Gospel to come to these other islands of the sea and proclaim the glad tiding to their brethren who are still in darkness,"[8] she wrote approvingly. A native presided over an impromptu dinner and showed his admiration

Whaling barks like the Addison *cruised all over the world in the 19th century. Cruises typically lasted two to five years, and the rewards for the ship's owners could be enormous.*

for Jehovah by intoning a blessing. "O Great Fader. Got no Moder, Got no Broder, Got no Sister. Make first de sea. Make first de dry land. Make first de moon and de stars. Make first de trees. Din he make man, and now Great Fader, give man he belly full. Amen." But Mary was skeptical as to how quickly the natives would see the light. "They are all great thieves; nothing can be left within their reach that they will not take."[9]

After a week, the *Addison* left Magdalena Island and continued a northern track through the Marquesas, stopping occasionally to trade for fruit and fresh meat. To this point, after four months, the ship had taken only two whales. There were no more to be seen before the *Addison* raised Maui on March 6, 1858.

Mary Lawrence had now been away from home for a year and a half. The short periods of time ashore had renewed her spirits and given her the opportunity to catch up on news and correspondence from her distant family. But the absence of whales and the unfilled oil casks in the hold of the *Addison* were a concern to both her and her husband. To return with less than 2,000 barrels of oil would be a great disappointment to the ship's owners. For Captain Lawrence, this cruise was his chance to redeem himself from the loss of the *Lafayette*. Things were not made better when they learned that the price of oil and bone had dropped considerably since they had left New Bedford. When they departed Hawaii in late-March, bound again for the summer whaling season in Alaskan waters, it was with the hope that this fourth leg of the the voyage would be more productive than the previous three.

The return to the Arctic and the Bering Sea proved to be a long and often frustrating cruise. Weather was not favorable with many days of fog and snow studded squalls. It was anything but summer. Rime ice on the decks and rigging greeted the crew in the mornings and large floating pieces of ice made navigation difficult and dangerous. The cabin stove was constantly going. The *Addison* struck a large piece of ice off Kamchatka in mid-June and was partially stove on the starboard side of the bow. Some good emergency carpentry work and the help of another ship's blacksmith, coupled with the quick use of pumps, kept the cold water out of the ship, but spirits were low as two months of hunting had seen the *Addison* take only two whales and less than two-hundred barrels of oil.

There were a number of whalers working the Cape Thaddeus grounds and Mary was able to occasionally gam with several of the ladies who were aboard their husband's ships. On one such visit, Minnie got a new kitten she named "Coda." Eskimos came on board and the little girl was the object of their attention. They wanted to hug and kiss her and she couldn't always avoid their embraces.

Sometimes as many as fifteen whaling vessels were in sight. As the cruise entered July most conversations between captains centered on how few whales had been taken. Discouragement was often reflected in Mary's journal. "Oh where shall whales be found?" she wondered on August 5th, and she noted that her husband was not sleeping well and was losing weight.

Late August was more productive and when the *Addison*, still leaking a bit from her encounter with the ice chunk, turned south for Hawaii in October, the ship had taken a total of seven whales and close to eight-hundred barrels of oil – about average for a summer cruise. The return to the Islands was, however, marred by the death of another boy named William Kalama who died from an extended illness despite the captain's application of medicine and "tonics." It was a somber crew that consigned the body of their shipmate to the deep on October 10th. They were off Diamond Head five days later on October 15, 1858.

Repairing the *Addison* from her encounter with the ice took several weeks. Because of this, the ship missed her scheduled departure for the New Zealand grounds and the decision was made to sail the shorter distance to the coast of Baja California where the California Gray Whales had a mating and birthing area. During the seven weeks in Honolulu, Mary enjoyed the company of many whaling wives and the additional spiritual comfort of Sabbath services at the missionary bethel there. When the ship put to sea in late-November she suffered from "boohoo" fever – something with malaria-like symptoms, and the melancholy that came with having probably too much time in contemplating her isolated state. But this cruise, if lacking in whales, saw quite a few ships in close proximity to the *Addison*. Many of these whalers had women and children aboard and Mary and Minnie had numerous occasions to go ashore and picnic on the wild and uninhabited coast of the Baja, as well as to host visitors in the *Addison*'s aft cabin. Her journal entries reflect genuine pleasure in the company

Classification of Whales

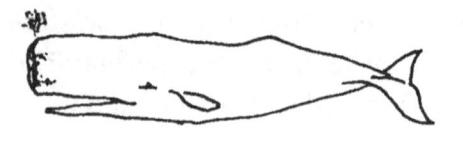

Sperm Whale

California Gray Whale

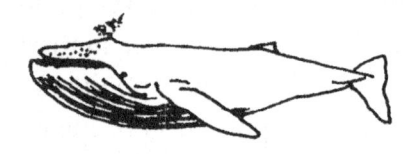

Humpback Whale

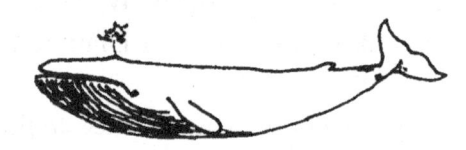

Sulphur-Bottom Whale

Bowhead Whale

Finback Whale

Right Whale

of a number of men and women who came aboard her floating home. Minnie continued her friendship with several playmates that she had met previously in Hawaii. Both females kept busy with a variety of activities both ashore and afloat. By the end of March, when the ship returned to the islands, the *Addison* had managed to take four whales and approximately two-hundred barrels of oil. It had not been a huge success, but as Mary noted, the *Addison* had not been "skunked" and the upcoming season in the Arctic held the possibility of filling their hold with oil so they could shape a course for Cape Cod.

They left Hawaii in late-April of 1859 for the Gulf of Alaska. This was the sixth cruise of the voyage and it took the ship into the Bering Sea and even as far north as the Arctic Ocean. Cold weather and foggy sea conditions, coupled with almost forty whaling ships in the area, made it difficult to capture any whales. Mary was having more trouble with her teeth and her husband gave her some laudanum for the pain. It was not until August 15th in the Bering Sea that the *Addison* took its first whale of that summer Arctic season. Visits from other captains indicated that no one else was having much luck. "Oh Dear!" she wrote a few weeks later, "Shall we ever get anything? That is my last thought when I go to sleep, and my first when I wake and also the burden of my dreams."[10]

With so many ships in close proximity, the whales could not seem to settle down and Captain Lawrence attempted, without success, to open some sea room between his ship and the others. They did take a second whale on August 23rd, but increasing ice floes made the hunt even more difficult. By the first week of September, snow squalls, gales, and driving sleet made it seem that the season would end early. On September 3rd, in heavy seas, while chasing a Bowhead, one of the ship's boats was stove by the wounded whale and twenty-year old Francis Lavarez drowned. The whale, which had been lanced by the boat, sank to

> 28th Saw nothing that looked like bow-heads through the morning, but an abundance of Muscle-diggers visible. A number of ships in sight – the greater part of them boiling. In the afternoon raised a bow-head and sent the boats out in pursuit of him. While they were out five or six made their appearance and we had the wonderful good fortune to capture one. We got him alongside about eleven P.M. So that we had more night work in cutting in, as Samuel was to be up through the night; I took Minnie in bed with me but as she could not come without "Billy Button" I had two bed fellows.

Mary Lawrence's journal shows a steady hand and an eye for detail. Her references to "muscle [sic.] diggers" is probably to Narwhals, a type of whale that uses a long tusk-like spear to free shellfish from the bottom. While the busy work of "cutting in" on a whale was going on at night, Mary snuggled below with two "bedfellows," Minnie and her doll, "Billy Button."

the bottom. Reflecting on the loss of the third crewman on the voyage, Mary wrote, "May it be a warning to us all to be prepared so that when the angel of death draws near, be it sooner or later, we may be found ready, one and all."[11]

The remaining two months in the Arctic saw much of the same pattern of bad luck. On September 16th, the *Addison* succeeded in putting two irons into a Bowhead but the whale sounded and took the lines with him. The same thing happened two days later with another whale. At last, on September 25th, the ship took whale number three which produced a solid 159 barrels. This, along with what had been taken earlier that summer, brought the total amount to about 460 barrels and close to seven-thousand pounds of bone – still not a particularly good amount. It was clear that unless something unusual happened in October, the cruise would have to be extended so that the *Addison* could approach the three thousand-barrel target desired by her owners.

October weather, unfortunately, made much of the final month impossible to hunt. A strong gale took away the Addison's main topsail on the 8th. "We have a heavy sea from all directions, and our good ship pitches, plunges, and rolls about in a way that would almost frighten a looker-on, especially in the squalls, which come very often today. I think this may be called the line gale, although it is rather late for it. At any rate it is the hardest gale we have experienced this voyage."[12] Realizing that continuing the cruise was probably not going to bring any more whales, Captain Lawrence set course for Hawaii and they arrived there on November 1st. It was here that fate delivered a final blow, for when the most recent New Bedford papers arrived on the island aboard the ship *Yankee*, Mary read of the death of her father in Sandwich. There had been no letters to give her any warning of her loss. "Shall I ever forget my sensations when the first paragraph on which my eyes rested was the death of my dear father. What a shock and how unexpected! Can it be that I have seen him for the last time? Oh, how fondly I have anticipated meeting Father, Mother, brothers, and sisters once more... With what a sad heart I shall return home. I feel as if his vacant place would be more than I can bear."[13]

The prospect of sailing for home did little to reduce the grief that Mary felt over her father's passing. That she had not been by his side when he died seemed to haunt her. As eager as she was to return to Cape Cod, her joy was diminished by the loss. The *Addison* sailed on December 2nd to work the New Zealand grounds one more time before heading home. For much of the month, her journal entries reflected little of significance. New Years' Day was spent on an idyllic atoll in the Cook Island chain. The crew gathered as much fruit as possible to sustain the voyage home. Mary busied herself in canning pineapples. On January 9th the *Addison* gamed with the whaler *Rambler* and Mary had a chance to visit with another female while Minnie played with the children. On the 16th they had another gam aboard the bark *Belle* and on the 20th it was the *James Arnold* out of New Bedford. Even if whales were scarce, Mary was, by these visits, at least able to escape the loneliness that was so much a part of extended sea time. Other incidents offered their own occasions for comment. The new steward mistakenly threw most of the silverware overboard in his rinsing pan so meals were eaten by sharing what few utensils remained. Mary worried about what she would do if she were to be called on to entertain visitors.

On February 11, 1860, the ship was hit by a gale that was so violent the cook had to prepare two meals. "If we can get our victuals to our mouths, we are fortunate," Mary wrote. "Before that, we are not sure of them. In shipping a sea, everything was taken from the stove by the roll of the ship – fish, potatoes, meat, and coppers all rolling around the deck together."[14] The heavy weather lasted the better part of a week. On February 25th the *Addison* made port in Akaroa, New Zealand.

The *Addison* stayed in Akaroa Harbor for about a week during which time Mary and Minnie had a number of opportunities to go ashore. The port was an excellent supplier of fruit and the crew brought as much on board as they could carry. Mary renewed some acquaintances and Minnie had the chance to play with other children during the time in port. On March 2nd, they put to sea once more in search of the elusive whales. After about a week of futility, Captain Lawrence decided it was time to turn for home. Mary, however, was still reflecting on the loss of her father and the change of course, coupled with the poor whaling results, did not brighten her spirits. "Samuel decided to give her sheet and let her go, so now we are in reality homeward bound. With what delight I would have hailed the sound had we taken three or four hundred barrels of oil and were I sure of meeting all whom I left behind; but that vacant chair rises before me, and my joy is changed to a flood of tears."[15]

It took several weeks of southeasterly sailing to reach the vicinity of Cape Horn. Snow squalls and heavy seas, combined with headwinds, made progress difficult and uncomfortable. On March 25th, a heavy gale commenced and the vessel lurched through the sea. "I thought I would have a luxury in the shape of stewed apple for sauce as we had a few apples left. So I prepared them. Borrowed a saucepan of the cook. Stewed them very nicely ... Was just preparing to take them up when there came an 'extra roll' which was a little more than I could manage and my apple sauce was splattered all around the cabin floor and the sauce pan went into the pantry. Consequently, our dinner was eaten minus the apple."[16]

The shorter days in these latitudes made it necessary to light the lamps by five o'clock in the afternoon. The passage around the Horn was, fortunately, without incident and they entered the Atlantic on April 12, 1860. By April 24th it was warm enough to do away with the cabin stove and the weather moderated. The crew began to straighten up the vessel and apply paint. It was customary for any returning whaler to look as smart as she could be when entering port and Captain Lawrence wanted his vessel to be presentable. Mary made it her business to clean the aft cabin and make her own quarters neat and bright. She paused in her cleaning to reflect on her four years at sea and gave a surprisingly positive summation to the voyage. "I shall feel badly, after all, to give up my *Addison* home. It would be folly to think of spending four years less happily than the last have been spent..."[17]

On May 13th, the *Addison* crossed the equator for the sixth time – two crossings in the Atlantic and four in the Pacific. One month later, on June 14th, the ship anchored in the Acushnet River outside New Bedford Harbor, home at last. The cruise had brought back about 2,500 barrels of oil and thousands of pounds of bone. With a profit of over $50,000, the owners of the ship were certainly satisfied and Captain Lawrence realized a share of approximately

$3,600 – a fair sum of money for that time. Most importantly for Mary, was that she, her husband, and her child were home again after surviving a challenging and often difficult adventure.

Captain Lawrence never made another whaling voyage. With the Civil War in its initial stages, he volunteered to serve as master of several cargo vessels that supplied the Union Army, and was so engaged during the war's duration. He continued at sea in various merchant commands after the war and died in 1892. Mary ended her sailing days with the conclusion of the *Addison* cruise, and outlived her husband by fourteen years. Little Minnie, the girl who passed her earliest years at sea, never married. She lived in Mohawk, New York for most of her life and died in 1923. All of the Lawrences are buried in the Oak Grove Cemetery in Falmouth. The *Addison* made several more whaling voyages, but was eventually lost in a storm off the Azores in 1875.

• • •

Chapter III

*"I thought that if they got too hungry, they'd
eat the cat before they started on me"*

Ulah Harding Reed of Chatham

Ulah Harding Reed was born on Old Harbor Road in Chatham. She was the daughter of Captain Samuel G. Harding. Her mother was Mary C. Clifford. At age nineteen she married Captain William E. Reed of Calais, Maine, master of the barkentine *Fred E. Richards*. The young bride first went to sea on a voyage to British Guiana carrying a load of ice and some general cargo. Other than an incident where her steward and the first mate got into a fight and the former came at her with a knife, she dismissed the voyage as uneventful. "Oh, there's always little things like that happening at sea," she later noted matter of factly in recalling the knife attack.

In the next several months, the *Richards* shuttled cargo and lumber between Florida and Georgia. She became used to the routine at sea and recalled, "I would sit on deck. There is always something interesting to observe. I'd watch the Mother Carey Chickens and follow the vessels in the distance. I'd watch the sailors work. I used to sew a good deal. I'd watch the stars and moon. That's where I learned to study the sky."[1]

In Wilmington, Delaware, while unloading a cargo of lumber,

the *Richards* developed a serious leak. The ship was taken to Philadelphia where it was hauled and caulked before loading coal for Havana, Cuba. In December of 1890, they put to sea. The voyage immediately encountered problems. "When we got off the Capes, we ran into a big storm. That strained the vessel and she began leaking again. We ran five days that way. The captain thought that he could save her... but when there was ten feet of water in the hold, he decided it was time to leave."[2]

At this point the *Richards* was almost four-hundred miles from land. Darkness was coming on and the sea was washing across the deck driven by the winter wind. Getting the nineteen-foot lifeboat launched was difficult. As it lay along side the stricken vessel, sometimes the lifeboat would be hull out of the water and it seemed that with each surge of the waves it might be battered to pieces. When Captain Reed went to the cabin to fetch her, Ulah decided that she couldn't leave her cat, Tottie, behind. After setting her pet pigeons free, she put the cat on her shoulders and made her way to the ship's rail. She later recalled her actions to save the cat, "I thoughht that if they got too hungry, they'd eat the cat before they started in on me."[3] One of the mates literally pitched her over the heaving rail into the lifeboat. The Captain, after making sure the running lights were on so the *Richards* would not be run down by another ship, was the last one to leave the vessel. At around 10:00 p.m. the survivors, who had stayed close to the hulk, heard a moaning-like sound and the Richards slipped beneath the waves.

When morning came, the twelve survivors surveyed the open ocean and saw not a single sail in sight. The sea continued to blow a gale and the captain had all he could do to keep the bow of the little craft into the wind to keep her from swamping. He broke a steering oar trying to hold her against the hard running current. Fortunately, because of their location in the Gulf Stream, the temperatures were not severe and they did not suffer from the cold. The captain's intent was to head for Abaco in the West

Indies but after several days the crew began to grumble that this island was too far away and that they should alter their course for Bermuda. Only with difficulty, and the fact that he had the only loaded pistol, did he convince the sailors that Abaco was their only realistic chance for a landfall.

As they drifted, they occasionally caught sight of ships on the horizon, but despite firing guns and flares they could not attract attention. One night, a steel-hulled passenger ship passed within a mile of them but it never noticed the small boat. Sharks trailed the lifeboat and snapped at the oars. Everyone had to bail to keep the boat afloat. Although the crew had taken some provisions with them, rations were meager and they survived on two pieces of hard bread, a swallow of water three times a day, and some canned beef every other day. Everyone was wet and started to develop salt water boils. When the seas ran high, Ulah was placed below the seats in the stern of the boat where she was soaked through by bilge water.

On the eighth day of their ordeal, a ship hove into view and they began to pull to intercept it. It was the Spanish bark *Felo* out of Barcelona, Spain. It took almost three hours of rigorous rowing before they were in hailing distance of the ship and finally spotted. Once aboard the rescuing vessel, the survivors were treated to hot meals and coffee. The Spanish captain graciously gave up his cabin to Captain Reed and Ulah. After five more days at sea, the survivors reached Brunswick, Georgia. When they arrived, it was Christmas morning.

In a letter that she wrote to her mother and father from Brunswick, Ulah expressed relief at having been rescued but a genuine sense of loss of her seagoing home. "I had just got her all fixed up and was as proud of her as I could be and was hoping that from Havana she would come to Boston as she probably would but she is gone and all my things with her. My chair which Papa gave me, my lace curtains and lace spread, my portiers and new carpet and everything. Will is pretty blue for fear that Carlton and Norward will say they want no more to do with him, but I don't see how they can blame him for when we left there was ten feet of water in her hold. I saved my three sets of wedding underclothes... I started with my new hat but it got soaked and blew away. I saved my photograph album but it got wet and fell all to pieces but did not spoil the photos."[4]

Captain Reed eventually did get another command and he and Ulah went to sea again a year later, this time to Rio De Janiero. The time after that, the captain headed to sea alone as she stayed home in Chatham with her family to have a baby girl. In 1893, they were at sea again, this time with the child, who survived a mild case of cholera during the voyage.

But Captain Reed, who had never fully recovered physically from the ordeal of losing the *Richards* and eight days in an open boat, was forced to give up his career at sea and he died in 1896. "He was never any good – all pulled to pieces inside," Ulah recalled. "They said he had consumption, but it wasn't that. It was the strain of being at that steering oar for eight days and nights."[5]

After her first husband's death, Ulah married Nathaniel J. Deer of Chatham. She divided her time between a residence in Cambridge, Massachusetts and her Chatham home on Seaview Street. When she died at age eighty-four on May 10, 1960, she was the oldest native-born Chatham resident.

• • •

Chapter IV

"Here we are, shipwrecked on a south sea island..."

PERSIS CROWELL ADDY OF DENNIS

A honeymoon voyage to the Far East turned into quite an adventure for twenty-eight year old Persis Crowell Addy of East Dennis. The daughter of prominent East Dennis clipper ship owner and master mariner, Prince Crowell, Persis married Captain John Henry Addy, a well respected deep water skipper from the same village. Captain Addy had been master of the clipper *Hippogriffe* and, at the time of the marriage, had just assumed command of the 648-ton clipper *Christopher Hall*. Both of these sleek vessels had been built in East Dennis in the Shiverick Shipyard.

In 1865, the couple left New York with a load of coal and merchandise, bound for Hong Kong. The letter that Persis sent to her parents on the eve of departure was indeed prophetic. "One would think," she wrote. "That I intended to be gone a dozen years or so by the fuss I make about it."[1] Certainly, there was cause for her to be excited. This would be Persis' first sea voyage and her first extended period away from her Cape Cod home. She had no idea that the trip would last for much longer than she had planned. Her story is not chronicled in a journal, but from a series of letters that

> LOSS OF A CAPE SHIP.—Advices from Tahiti, to May 5, report the total loss of ship Christopher Hall, of Dennis, upon Navigator's Island. She sailed from Howland's Island, Nov. 24, for Boston, with a cargo of guano. The C. H. was a ship of 648 tons register, built at Dennis in 1857, was owned by P. S. Crowell and others of Dennis and vicinity, and commanded by Capt. John H. Addy.

From the Yarmouth Register, May 31, 1867.

she sent home to her family. And they became the main source of what happened to her. She confessed to her mother in one of those communications that journal keeping was not something that she wanted to do. "I suppose it would be well to keep a journal for your especial benefit," she wrote. "But since I have read Mr. [Henry Ward] Beecher's definition of a journal, I have not felt inclined to write one. He calls a journal 'the Devil's vanity trap.'"

After traveling much of the summer of 1866 between Akyab, Burma, and the Chinese port of Shanghai and British Hong Kong, where Persis enjoyed the company of other Cape Codders who were engaged in the Far Eastern trade,[2] the ten-year old *Christopher Hall* set a course east for Howland's Island to load guano for eventual delivery to the Pacific Guano factory in Woods Hole, Falmouth. Sailing through the Navigator Islands near Apia in Western Samoa, the ship struck an uncharted reef in January of 1867 and began to sink. Persis could save only a small bag of clothing and her watches and chains. In a steady rain and with a high sea running, the crew fastened a rope around her waist and lowered her into the lifeboat. As water sloshed in the small boat, she helped bail by using an old hat until someone handed her a bucket, making her task a bit easier. Fortunately, they were fairly close to a small island and were able to make a landfall witthout much difficulty.

As they approached the small atoll, there was concern that it might be inhabited by unfriendly natives. There were several cases in the area where shipwrecked mariners had been attacked by bloodthirsty tribes and the crew held their weapons at the ready for any possible threat.

"When we neared the shore we espied little huts," Persis wrote in a letter sent to her parents shortly after landfall. "And four women whose only dress was leaves fastened around their hips, and long enough to reach their knees. We by no means felt sure of a kind reception but decided to land. The natives appeared very kindly disposed, shook hands with us and led us to their chief's hut. The chief spread clean mats for us to sit on, which I can assure you, I was very glad to do."[3]

For days, the survivors adapted as best they could to the conditions of the small island, eating tropical fruits, fish, and occasional meat. Persis made herself as comfortable as possible but made it clear that style had its limits. "...I did not want to put on a gentleman's entire suit, or even to adopt the native women's costume."[4]

Word of the survivors' predicament was eventually sent to the port of Apia, the main harbor in Samoa, and they were picked up by some Europeans and given quarters there with an American man who had taken an island woman for a wife. "I am well now, and with kind people, Henry has dropsy, is under a physician's care, and improving... We do not know how we shall get home but think we shall go in the Brig *Susanna* to Hamburg, which will leave here in three or four weeks."[5] She was apologetic that she would not be able to bring her nephew "Brinnie" any souvenirs of the voyage, but she wanted him to know that she would tell him some good stories about the little boys and girls on Apia when she returned home.

Finally, after more than a month and a half, Persis and her husband were able to make the journey back to Cape Cod via Europe. For Captain Addy, the voyage proved to be his last. Never fully recovering from the ordeal, and in weakened health, "Henry" developed consumption and died in East Dennis in the fall of 1867. He was forty years old.[6] Persis did not remarry and lived in the family home on Center Street. Some time later, while temporarily living with her close friend Reverend Anna Howard Shaw in Hingham, she developed a brain tumor. She died at age forty-one in March of 1878. She and her husband are both buried in the Sea Street cemetery in East Dennis.

• • •

Persis Crowell Addy. Courtesy of Jim Carr.

Chapter V

*"You speak lie,
we kill you all three."*

LUCY LORD HOWES OF DENNIS

One of the most incredible sea experiences of Cape Cod women is the story of how Lucy Lord Howes of Dennis survived the horrible murder of her husband at the hands of Chinese pirates while on board the hermaphrodite brig *Lubra*. The tale is one of courage and determination exhibited by a young mother suddenly thrown into a situation where her life and the lives of her two small chily-six year old Lucy Howes is based on a letter written to her sister from Hong Kong in October 1866, about a month after the ordeal. The full text of the letter can be found on page two in the *Yarmouth Register* newspaper, for Friday, January 18, 1867.

Lucy Lord Howes had just finished dinner on September 23, 1866. The weather had been nice enough so that she and her husband, Captain Benjamin Perkins Howes, had been able to eat on deck rather than taking their meal in the stuffy cabin below. The *Lubra* was outbound from Hong Kong and headed for Yokohama, Japan. In addition to the family, the ship was manned by two mates, five seamen, a Chinese cook and a Chinese steward. As they sat on the aft deck house, Lucy held her two-year old

Lucy Lord Howes.
Courtesy of the Dennis Historical Society.

daughter, Carrie. Her youngest child, four-month old Jennie, who had been born aboard in May, was being cared for by a nurse. A single Chinese junk sailed into view and approached the *Lubra* and hailed her as to her destination. Asked if they wanted a harbor pilot, Captain Howes indicated that he did not and warned the Chinese vessel away. Instead of standing off, the junk closed on the American brig and about a dozen pirates rushed the vessel and climbed aboard. Several crewmen were immediately killed while attempting to resist. There was a brief struggle but the *Lubra*'s crew was disorganized and soon overwhelmed by the raiders.

Quickly scooping up little Carrie, Captain Howes escorted Lucy below to the main cabin. Now in full command of the ship, the pirates signaled that they wanted to parlay. They indicated that if the captain would cooperate and hand over any gold or opium, they would leave the survivors unharmed and depart with their booty. Believing that he had no alternative, Captain Howes allowed the pirates into his cabin. When he told them that there was no gold on board nor was there any opium, the pirates became enraged. "You speake lie!" They screamed. "We kill you all three!"

The pirates began to ransack the ship for whatever valuables they could find. Repeatedly they came back to the captain's cabin demanding to know where the gold and opium was hidden. With drawn swords and pistols, the invaders menaced the trio, at one point striking Captain Howes with the flat of their swords.

"The pirates helped themselves to anything they wanted in the cabin, such as what money they could find, together with articles of jewelry, wines, etc.," Lucy recalled in her letter home. "...We both sat on the sofa with little Carrie between us, she asleep a part of the time. We both fanned her to keep her quiet. I asked Benjamin if he thought we would have to go through the same scene again. He answered that he could give me no courage to the contrary. He did not seem to think they would kill me and the children, at least, but we made up our minds to meet our fate and all go together.

The Lubra *has been referred to as a clipper brig. In fact, she was a hermaphrodite grig, sometimes called a barkentine. With only two masts.* Lubra *had a square rigged foremast and a schooner-like fore-and-aft mainsail and gaff topsail on the mainmast.*

We both hoped to be shot, as that seemed the most merciful way of being killed."

This cat and mouse game continued throughout the night until, as dawn arrived, the pirates made ready to depart. At this point, Lucy believed that there was at least a possibility that the three of them would be spared. Baby Jennie, who was above decks with her nurse, she imagined, had probably already been killed and her body thrown overboard. The chief of the pirates suddenly came into the cabin where Lucy, Benjamin, and Carrie were sitting. As the pirate drew his pistol, Captain Howes said to Lucy, "It is our fate, Lucy, and we must meet it." A few minutes later a single shot rang out killing the Captain. "I dropped on Benjamin's shoulder and let the blood flow over me, at the same time holding down Carrie, for I fancied he had come to dispatch us. I lifted my head and told him to shoot me. He lighted a small piece of candle and sat it within a few inches of my head on the table (I believe he thought me wounded) and then went on deck." In the dim light, the pirates apparently believed that they had killed the entire family and they left the cabin and reboarded their own ship.

As she lay next to her husband, Lucy searched for any signs of life but could find none. Holding Carrie close to her and hushing the child, she listened to the sound of the departing men. In a final act, one of the pirates heaved a heavy block of wood through the cabin window, glancing off Lucy and striking Carrie on the head. Despite fear and pain, Lucy continued to lie very still to convince the pirates that they had killed her. And then all was quiet.

Not long after, there was a sound above deck. Cautiously, Lucy opened the hatch and was surprised to see one of the crewmen who had apparently hidden himself at the outset of the melee. She told him that Captain Howes was dead and asked who else had survived. "Mr. Hall, the mate is dead, but there are two men beside myself alive," he reported. As she emerged on deck, she heard the cry of an infant coming from near the capstan on the top-gallant forecastle. Incredibly, it was baby Jennie, unharmed and bawling for something to eat. They nurse had apparently been thrown overboard or had been taken away by the pirates, but the infant had survived.

Before they departed, the pirates set fires on the *Lubra* and opened the ship's supply of gunpowder, intending to blow her up. Lucy and the survivors worked furiously to put the fires out and save the ship. It was at this point that the first mate, twenty-two year old Henry Hall, appeared from his hiding place up forward. At the outset of the attack he had run toward the bow and had

Hong Kong gravesite of Captain Benjamin Perkins Howes and baby Jenny. Courtesy of Jim Carr.

secreted himself in a deep and narrow locker under the top-gallant forecastle. The space, which was filled with fence pickets, allowed him to conceal hp and narrow locker under the top-gallant forecastle. The space, which was filled with fence pickets, allowed him to conceal himself even as the pirates made a thorough search of the ship. Hearing them depart, he had emerged to find the few surviving crewmen and his captain's wife and two children.[1]

The small group put out the fires and was able to jury rig a sail and make for Hong Kong. Lucy eventually changed out of her bloodstained clothing and spent much of the next day sitting near the ship's wheel in her rocking chair, holding Carrie in her arms, with Jennie asleep in her cradle by her side. Lucy could not sleep and did not return to the cabin where her husband's body lay undisturbed.

When they reached port and told their story, Lucy secured a temporary berth aboard an American ship the *A.M. Lawrence*. The captain of that ship, Gorham Taylor Jr., of Yarmouth, had known Captain Howes and he graciously gave up his quarters on the ship until early December, at which time Lucy moved to a boarding house for the remainder of her stay in Hong Kong. She was given much attention and sympathy by the European and American community in the Chinese port and hundreds of people attended Captain Howes' funeral. She was asked by authorities to remain in Hong Kong until the pirates were caught and identified. Not long after, they were apprehended and, with Lucy's testimony, tried and hanged for their crime. The fate of the *Lubra* might be explained by the fact that the ship carried, in addition to her cargo of general merchandise, a supply of arms and ammunition. In the investigation that followed the tragedy, evidence was presented that some of the Chinese stevedores had alerted the pirates to the presence of the weapons and this, rather than the desire for gold or opium, may have been the real motive for the raid. To further compound Lucy's tragedy, the infant Jennie picked up a sickness in Hong Kong and died on November 12th. The child was buried there beside her father in Happy Valley.

On January 15, 1867, Lucy Lord Howes and little Carrie took passage on the ship *Portland* and sailed for New York, arriving there on April 14, 1867. A few days later she was home in Dennis. She remained there with various relatives and occasionally traveled to Maine to visit other relatives. In November of 1868, Lucy married Sylvester Hooper and they resided in South Berwick, Maine where she raised a second family. By 1886, she and Sylvester had separated (or divorced) and she had moved to Brockton, Massachusetts, where she resided until around 1909 when she homesteaded out west to Oregon. There she finished her days on

November 5, 1926. She is buried in Roseburg, Oregon. As for little Carrie, she later married a cousin, Charles Wesley Howes II, and after living in Brockton, Massachusetts for a time, also went west to Oregon where she joined her mother. After working as a nurse in Roseburg, she moved to San Diego, California, where she spent the rest of her life, until her death there at age ninety-three.

• • •

Chapter VI

"A grand old pile beyond anything I had imagined."

REBECCA WOOD HOWES
OF SOUTH YARMOUTH

These were the words used by Rebecca Wood Howes, the wife of Captain Barnabas C. Howes, to describe her visit to Windsor Castle while on an around-the-world trip with her husband in 1875. Sailing aboard the clipper ship *Swallow*, Rebecca enjoyed the company of her husband and the excitement of seeing some of the more exotic sights of the world on a voyage that took a little over a year.

The trip took her to London, Scandinavia, Australia, Hong Kong, Japan, and finally to San Francisco, where she would board the newly completed transcontinental railroad for the final leg back to Boston and Cape Cod. The record of her trip was compiled in her journal and edited by the late Anne Baxter of Stratford, Connecticut. I was given a transcribed copy of the journal by Jane Baxter of Centerville, and I am indebted to the family for letting me use the source in tracing the journey of this well educated and very literate woman. All of the quotes in this chapter are from the transcribed journal.[1]

By way of background, Rebecca Wing Wood was the daughter of Orlando and Margaret Wood of South Yarmouth. She married Barnabas Howes in 1869. The marriage eventually produced three children – Margaret, Willis, and Cyrus. Numerous references indicate that both Captain Howes and Rebecca were members of the Quaker community of South Yarmouth and, no doubt, attended services in the small meeting house there in what was then called "Quaker Village." At the time of the voyage, Rebecca was thirty-three years old.

The clipper ship *Swallow* was an older vessel, having been built in East Boston in 1854. She was typical of her class, displacing over 1,400 tons, and with a length of 210 feet. The *Swallow* was a well respected veteran of the Far East trade and had a long and profitable career of over thirty years before she eventually sank in an Atlantic storm in 1885. A fast sailor, the *Swallow* typically made runs from San Francisco to New York in approximately 110 to 120 days on the average – considered very good time in the age of sail.[2]

The spring of 1875 had been unusually cold on Cape Cod. Rebecca recorded that the laundry that she hung up outside of her house on Bellevue Avenue in South Yarmouth was frozen on the line as late as mid-April and snow had fallen on the 13th. But the peepers were chirping and the first blossoms of apple trees were in view as she boarded the train at the South Yarmouth depot on May 10th. A telegram had arrived earlier in the month from Captain Howes instructing her to meet him in England so they could sail together. It would have been an entirely pleasant day if she had not boarded the Cunard steamer *Scotia* in New York knowing that she would be missing the company of her beloved mother in South Yarmouth. Margaret and her daughter were almost like sisters. Theirs was a relationship that was perhaps made all the closer because Rebecca's husband was frequently away at sea. In fact, during the first three years of their marriage, she and Barnabas had only shared a total of three months together. Even when he was home he was often

Rebecca Wood Howes. Courtesy of Jane Baxter.

Captain Barnabas C. Howes. Courtesy of Jane Baxter.

preoccupied with business matters. Now he was in Liverpool, England with the *Swallow*, waiting for her to join him. Rebecca expected to be gone for about a year but it was never a certainty as to when a voyage would be completed. As she sat in her cabin on the eve of departure aware that she would be the only woman aboard the transatlantic steamer, she wrote about her "utter loneliness." But a day later, the feelings of loneliness had been supplanted by something more pressing – the almost universal experience of seasickness. For several days, Rebecca took only light soup and stayed below in an attempt to settle her stomach.

The weather was pleasant enough as the steamer passed into the Gulf Stream. The ship was making a good twelve knots aand Rebecca had gained her sea legs and was enjoying walks around the deck in the company of several passengers. Other than a few rainy days, the passage to Liverpool was a comfortable and pleasant experience. She noted the sighting of land off the Irish coast on May 20th and of signaling at Mizzen Head and Fastnet Light on the same day. The *Scotia* took the pilot on board in the late afternoon of May 21st and Rebecca happily greeted her husband when he came aboard to get her the next morning.

Captain Howes and Rebecca took the train from Liverpool to London where they secured lodging in a hotel there. One of the first things the couple did, before settling into these temporary quarters, was to locate the nearest Quaker meeting house in the city. They attended services there on Sunday, May 23rd, and spent the rest of the day visiting nearby Greenwich. For the next three weeks Rebecca had the pleasure of touring London with other families from Cape Cod whose ships were also in port.

Like any modern tourist, Rebecca took advantage of shopping and sightseeing while in London. When he was not conducting ship's business in Liverpool, Captain Howes accompanied her to various attractions. They visited the National Art Gallery and Windsor Castle. On Thursday, May 27th, they joined another captain and

The Clipper Ship Swallow, *painted by a Chinese artist in Hong Kong. Courtesy of Jane Baxter.*

his wife and spent the afternoon at Crystal Palace. "...we wandered about all the afternoon enjoying the lovely grounds reminding me some of Central Park" she wrote. "...was much pleased with the views of Pompeii and the Alhambra."

Shopping excursions in Picadilly, where Rebecca had some dresses made, were sandwiched around other visits to the city's highlights. She was impressed by the British houses of Parliament at Westminster and recorded seeing the grave of British poet Oliver Goldsmith. The couple visited a number of art galleries and the British Museum and took a boat ride on the Thames River. She commented on seeing the Tower of London and sitting in the cell once occupied by Sir Walter Raleigh. In the final week in London, in between packing and writing letters, Rebecca visited the Albert Memorial and she and her husband took in a concert at the Royal Albert Hall.

On June 17th the *Swallow* set sail for Sweden. The North Sea brought back some feelings of discomfort and Rebecca spent the first few days at sea below in her cabin sewing with her new sewing machine. "Rougher than we've had it and I have felt quite uncomfortable for the most of the day but have managed to go to the table to the three meals tho' eating very little," she wrote. Headwinds, a strong current, and a cold rain made the trip into the Baltic Sea difficult and Rebecca continued to have an unsettled stomach. The rainbow that she mentioned on June 26th seemed to do little to brighten up her spirits.

The ship's destination was the Swedish port of Sundsvall on the Gulf of Bothnia. They reached it on Friday, July 9, 1875. The *Swallow* was tied up in this small harbor community for about a month. The town was a far cry from London and Rebecca had to content herself with sewing and several berry picking excursions to the nearby countryside. There were no Quaker meeting houses in Sweden and she spent quiet Sundays reading aboard ship. The weather was cold and rainy for much of the time and this, coupled with the frequent absence of her husband as he tended to business, did little to dispel her frequent references to loneliness. She expressed no great remorse at seeing Sundsvall recede over the stern on August 10th.

Denmark proved to be a much more interesting stop and, after leaving the *Swallow* in Elsinore (Helsingor), Rebecca and her husband took the two-hour train ride to Copenhagen. Rebecca enjoyed the beautiful countryside and commented on the farming activities and the flower gardens. Arrriving in the city at 9:00 a.m., they commenced seeing the sights of the Danish capital. After touring the Thorvaldsons Museum and having dinner at the Hotel D'Angle-terre, followed by a evening walk through the Tivoli, they returned to Elsinore, arriving near midnight.

Exhausted from all this activity, Rebecca stayed in Elsinore until Monday, August 23rd, when she again took the train to

Copenhagen, joining several other captains' wives for a final tour of the city. On Wednesday morning, August 25th, she was back on board the *Swallow* and was once again at sea.

Unlike the previous short legs of her journey, the next segment of her trip on board the *Swallow* would take more than four months. The new destination was Australia and they would not arrive there until early December. For the next 120 days, Rebecca's journal is filled with reflections on the weather, the state of the sea, latitude and longitude positions, and the mentioning of occasional "speakings" with other vessels that would temporarily break the overall monotony of the long sea voyage. Her activities during this time included sewing, reading, and ironing. That the monotony of sailing across a seemingly endless ocean could occasionally fray the edges of matrimonial harmony can be seen in her entry of September 23rd: "...To me this has been a dark day ended by an unsatisfactory talk with Barna. May I live nearer to thee oh God in the days to come." And another entry on the following day, "Fair wind and very pleasant but oh I have been so sad."

Rebecca recorded a solar eclipse on September 29, 1875 while sailing near the Canary Islands. *Swallow* spoke the ship *Borelia* out of Cardiff bound for Aden on October 5th and the bark *Garland* out of Liverpool on the 7th. They crossed the Equator on October 10th. Approaching the Cape of Good Hope and the southern tip of Africa near the end of October, the ship encountered headwinds and heavy swells. "Ship still rolling from side to side making it impossible to work as often having to hold myself where I am,," she wrote. "...with Barna's assistance took a little walk on the [deck] house." Much of November continued "squally and rainy." Rebecca resumed her sewing and completed pajamas, slippers, and several dresses. At last, they sighted land on Thursday, December 2, 1875. It was Kangaroo Island just off South Australia. On December 4th, the *Swallow* took a pilot off Port Adelaide and was towed into Melbourne.

After four months at sea, putting feet on dry land was a pleasure. The couple took the train into the city and were met by Captain William Howes and his wife. They booked a room at the Guardian Hotel and commenced touring the city. After several days at the Guardian, Rebecca and her husband took new quarters at the Ford Hotel. Afternoons were spent with several women that she had met in other ports and they busied themselves while the men did business at the waterfront. Rebecca mentions having attended the races with her husband. A short bout with stomach flux caused by bad food put her in bed for a few days, but she still managed to occasionally go to the beach and have tea with a number of her female friends. What is not mentioned in the journal is the fact that Rebecca was in the early stages of pregnancy and this probably explains numerous references of feeling ill and her needing to rest. On December 13th she wrote, "This morning Barna gave me a big dose of oil. The first time I have been to the medicine chest. Hope it may effect a cure." Typical of the times, and common in most female seagoing journals, she did not mention her pregnancy at any time in the entire journal. Victorian women viewed pregnancy almost as an illness and rarely discussed their condition with candor. They used various euphemisms which gave hints of what they were experiencing, but preferred silence on any matters connected with sexual activity. Pregnancy was something to be "gotten over."

There was a Quaker community in Melbourne and the couple were pleased to be able to attend services there. Christmas Day saw her entertaining guests and serving a plump roast goose. Rebecca made a cake for the occasion and pronounced it "passably good." The arrival of several American ships in December increased her circle of female friends and the rest of January 1876 was pleasantly spent in the company of other shipmasters and their wives. She was back on board *Swallow* on January 24th and the ship left Melbourne the next day.

After a three-week stop at Newcastle, north of Sydney, where the vessel was loaded with wool, the ship's course was set for Hong Kong. *Swallow* put into the Tasman Sea on February 27th and immediately ran into a heavy gale. After spending the better part of three months ashore, it took some time for Rebecca to regain her sea legs. On February 28th she wrote, "A sick day lying about all day and the ship laboring hard with a rough sea." But within a short time, she was back to her sewing and embroidery work even if her stomach still gave her occasional moments of discomfort. After a fifty-seven day passage north through the Caroline and Mariana Island chain, and recrossing the Equator into the East China Sea, *Swallow* arrived at Hong Kong on Sunday, April 23, 1876.

In Hong Kong, the ship was immediately surrounded by Chinese sampans eager to trade. A number of Chinese were allowed on board the *Swallow* bringing chickens and vegetables. Captain Howes and Rebecca left the ship in the afternoon and boarded rickshaws for a tour of the city gardens. As she reflected on the day, Rebecca seemed a bit concerned that there was no formal observation of the Sabbath. "The streets seemed very noisy and full of Chinese," she wrote. "Their stores all open, nothing of Sabbath quiet."

Rebecca was pleased to note that Captain Benjamin Bray of Yarmouth and his wife had arrived in Hong Kong at the same time in their ship *Comet*. The two Cape couples enjoyed catching up on the news from home. They visited the Kowloon section of the city and searched for shells along the beach there. On May 7th they made an excursion to the English cemetery on the edge of the city and located the grave of Captain Benjamin Perkins Howes of Dennis who had been murdered aboard his ship *Lubra* by Chinese pirates in 1866. Shopping and entertaining other American captains and their wives occupied much of the remainder of the month.

By this time, Rebecca was almost six months pregnant and her husband was concerned that she might have a difficult time with the birth of her first child while aboard ship. *Swallow* still had considerable time at sea ahead and a port call in Antwerp, Netherlands before finishing the cruise. After some discussion, the decision was made to send Rebecca back to Cape Cod by steamship so that she could have her baby at home in familiar surroundings. That this was not an easy decision can be seen in her journal entries made as she packed for the long trip that she would take alone. On May 15, 1876 she left *Swallow* for the last time. "A rainy day and with a heart of sadness and tearful eyes, I leave the *Swallow*, so long my home, and come to the steamer *City of Peking*. Barnabas with me til the steamer is ready to sail, three o'clock – a long lonesome eve."

From Hong Kong, the 5,000-ton *City of Peking* traveled to Yokohama, Japan, arriving for a short port stay on Monday, May 22nd. Rebecca was uncomfortable and not feeling well and spent much of the voyage alone in her cabin. Her waking time was occupied in sewing with an occasional break for a foray up to the ship's saloon where she sat and talked with other women who were also headed home to the United States. When the weather was good and she felt up to it she walked the outside deck to take in the salt air. But not being near her husband made her quite lonely and her journal reflects her isolation. When the steamer reached Japan, many of her new friends left the ship. She missed their company, noting, "Then one after another of the passengers went on shore till I was left quite alone and so lonesome."

On the second day in Yokohama she did go ashore in the company of the ship's Purser. She was feeling well enough to "visit a number of curio shops where there were beautiful things, rode in a Jinriksha – a big baby carriage – went to the bluffs getting a nice view of the harbor and was back to the ship at 'tiffin' (lunch) having had a very satisfactory glimpse of Yokohama." The new passengers embarked on the *City of Peking*, however, apparently didn't make a favorable impression on Rebecca. She noted on the day of sailing from Yokohama that she "spent the evening in [the] Social Hall but found there an unsocial company." This continued and she retreated to her cabin for much of the rest of the seventeen-day passage to San Francisco.

In San Francisco, Rebecca was met by her brother-in-law, Cyrus Howes, and went across the bay to Oakland where she took a room at the Tubbs Hotel. Being on land and in the company of a member of her family and some other friends revived her spirits. She went into San Francisco and did some shopping and spent two late evenings with friends, catching up with news from Cape Cod. After just three days she was ready to board the transcontinental railroad for the cross country trip back to her home in Yarmouth. She left Oakland alone on June 13th and traveled east in a hot and crowded railroad car. Always willing to engage strangers in conversation, Rebecca quickly made several new friends as the cars passed through the dry plains of the far west. At Sherman, Wyoming, when the train stopped for water, her curiosity over "specimens" that she was collecting to bring home almost caused her to miss the train when it started to move without her. She reached Chicago on Sunday, June 18th, where she was again met by family friends. The train arrived in Boston on Tuesday, June 20th, where her cousin Emily greeted her and, after a few hours delay, she boarded the Cape train at the Old Colony Depot. Four hours later she was greeted by her mother and family friends in South Yarmouth.

On July 25, 1876, about a month after returning home, Rebecca gave birth to her first child, Margaret, who was named after her mother. Her husband Barnabas didn't get home to see his wife and new daughter until almost a year later. This was the only sailing trip that Rebecca would make. Much of the next twenty years were spent at the house on Bellevue Avenue, raising the three children while her husband continued his voyages around the world. In 1885, almost ten years after this voyage, *Swallow*, now under new command, sprang a leak on her passage from Liverpool, England, to Sydney, Australia. With the pumps choked by seawater, the ship was abandoned at sea without loss of life. Captain Howes died a few years later in San Francisco on March 7, 1892 from injuries that he suffered when struck by a cable car. Rebecca passed away only six years later on September 28, 1898. She was fifty-six years old. Both are buried together in the Howes family cemetery off Beach Street in Dennis.

• • •

Chapter VII

"...Santa Claus never visits the west coast of Africa unless he comes in the shape of an Arab..."

CLARA COOK RYDER OF PROVINCETOWN

Women from Provincetown in the mid-nineteenth century not only lived at the ocean's doorstep, but many of them also experienced the routine of life at sea with their sea captain husbands. The Cape tip was the leading port in Barnstable County, with a large number of whaling and merchant vessels sailing from there. At one time there were over sixty whaleships homeported in Provincetown, making it second only to New Bedford in Massachusetts as a whaling center.

Clara Cook Ryder was born at Orland, Maine on February 22, 1830. She moved to Cape Cod as a young girl and eventually married Captain Stephen A. Ryder, a Provincetown native and prominent ship owner. Her first extended sea experience was in 1857 aboard the whaling bark *N.D. Chase* and it took her on a two-year voyage into the Atlantic Ocean and later into the Indian Ocean.[1] During her time at sea, Clara kept a journal that reflected her days on board. In it we see a lively and sensitive woman who chronicled the variety of activities that came with the pursuit of whales. And we can also see a wife and mother who struggled to manage and control her two small sons on a pitching deck while attempting to make a comfortable home at sea for her husband.[2]

On June 8, 1857, after an evening of going away parties and tearful farewells with friends and family, Clara Cook Ryder sat in her sea cabin with her two sons, Elijah Thomas Ryder who was five years old, and her "bunny," Frank Bunchina Ryder, who was two. As the ship weighed anchor in Provincetown, she could see people gathered along the waterfront to bid them goodbye. A small flotilla of friends sailed alongside the *N.D. Chase* as she hoisted sail and moved away from her anchorage. The outbound leg around Long Point was filled with both melancholy and excitement at the prospect of crossing the broad Atlantic Ocean in search of whales. Other than occasional short coastal voyages, Clara had never been away from home for an extended period. At age twenty-seven she had no long sea voyage experience to draw on and she was entering a world that was certainly alien to her. The fact that her two small boys were aboard was both a comfort and a responsibility. The care of active children was enough to occupy any parent on land, never mind in the rough environs of a whaling ship. She looked at them and wondered how two years away from home would affect their lives. Off Race Point a boat came close enough to hoist over fifteen fresh lobsters for the crew and then after some last shouts of goodbye, Clara watched as the land, and the only home she had ever really known, disappeared astern.

Within the first two weeks Clara and the boys had gotten over their seasickness and had settled into a seagoing routine. Occasionally, the crew took to the boats when a whale was spotted, but none were taken. For Clara, the day's activities were centered on things she would have done at home. "I knit all day with the exception of taking care of the children," she noted on June 23rd. She was feeling well enough to venture around the deck in good weather and to try her hand at assisting the steward in making bread and washing dishes. The excitement of seeing occasional

*Captain Stephen A. Ryder, Clara Cook Ryder and "Bunny".
Courtesy of Mrs. Ralph Manning.*

passing vessels on the horizon broke the otherwise monotonous movement of the *N.D. Chase* in her eastward course toward the Azores and she noted their presence in her journal.

On July 1st, after a "squally"passage with the sails often reefed, the *N.D. Chase* reached the Azores and the island of Flores. In the harbor at Santa Cruz was the schooner *John Adams* of Provincetown, Captain Doyle, Master, and a second vessel, the schooner *Silver Cloud* out of New London, Connecticut.[3] The weather was comfortable and Clara took the boys and went ashore where the children were given canary birds and some rabbits to take back to the ship Clara took the boys and went ashore where the children were given canary birds and some rabbits to take back to the ship as pets. Captain Ryder busied himself in trading with the islanders for potatoes, onions, cloves, oranges, eggs, turkeys, and other staples. One of the mates had to see the English doctor

Atlantic whalers cruised the islands from the Azores to Cape Verde. This was a common scene in the nineteenth centurt as a whaler "cuts in" a whale carcass to prepare the blubber for the "try pots" aboard the ship.
Courtesy of Cape Cod Community College.

there for treatment of an ulcerated tooth. On July 4th, Clara acted as a hostess to several captains on board the *N.D. Chase* and supervised a turkey dinner as part of the Independence Day celebration. She noted that the experience had been enjoyable and she was as satisfied "...as if I had been at home with the exception of the society of my friends..."

Sailing around the island chain, often with the schooner *John Adams* in sight, the *N.D. Chase* took several blackfish but they were unable to bring any large whales in. They anchored off Pico and Clara sent her first letters home via a departing ship there. Fresh fruit from the island provided a good variation in the ship's diet. On July 15th the ship sailed for St. Georges Island where Captain Ryder traded some of the blackfish oil for produce. A few days later at Praya, on the island of Terciera, Clara went ashore and met some English speaking women and spent an enjoyable afternoon conversing before returning to her shipboard home later that evening.

Once back at sea, the job of preserving some of the fruit had to be completed and Clara busied herself with making sure that all of the bartered produce was properly stored below decks. "I cut up some apricots and tried to dry them in the sun but they would not dry and I stewed them and they made a beautiful sauce." She sewed and ironed clothes for the children and watched as the crew engaged in regular "ship's duty." That she was not neglecting her mind can be seen in her note, "I knit some and read the life and beauties of Fanny Fern loaned to me by Captain Doyle."

During their time of sailing among the islands in the Azores chain, the *N.D. Chase* and her crew were on the alert for whales. While they spotted an occasional creature, they were unsuccessful in taking any of them. Other than the initial catch of blackfish, which yielded very little oil, the ship remained "clean" throughout the summer. Clara's journal mentions other ships working in their vicinity. In addition to the *John Adams*, there were the New

Bedford whalers *Tropic Bird* and *Majestic,* the bark *Grayhound* of Westport, Massachusetts, the *Richard Clark* out of Bath, Maine, and the *Silver Cloud* of New London, Connecticut.

In late-August, Clara recorded the first real instance of stormy weather. A gale started to blow on the 21st and continued for several days. The ocean swells added to the discomfort aboard the ship. She and the boys were seasick again. "Everything in great confusion," she wrote on August 23rd. "All moveable things have to be lashed to keep them in their places." The next day as the storm played itself out, she noted, "Impossible for me or the children to go around the deck without help." Four days later the weather had turned calm and Clara remarked about having fried porpoise for breakfast as her routine – and her stomach, returned to normal.

On September 1, 1857, the *N.D. Chase* spoke the bark *Cherokee* of Greenock, Scotland. Again acting as hostess, Clara made sure that Captain Cowans of the Scottish vessel enjoyed his meal of stuffed turkey and mince pie. Captain Cowans reciprocated by inviting Clara on board his own vessel and presenting her with a dozen bottles of claret wine and some books. He sent along a box of sweetmeats for the two boys.

With no whales taken in over three months, Clara was still upbeat enough about the ship's prospects that she wrote a note of encouragement to herself and the crew. "Nothing to be seen but our own bark as she sails through the ruffled sea and now and then fetching a heavy lurch," she entered on September 17th. "But it avails us nothing to murmur, for all in good time a spouter will come along and then hurrah boys we will soon have him alongside [and] strip him of his choicest portion [and] put it into oily operation and then stow it away in the hold. So three cheers for the bark *N.D. Chase* and her jolly crew."

Believing that it might do some good to spend a bit of time ashore, Captain Ryder brought the ship to Fayal on September 22nd for a few days of relaxation. Clara was pleased to see the

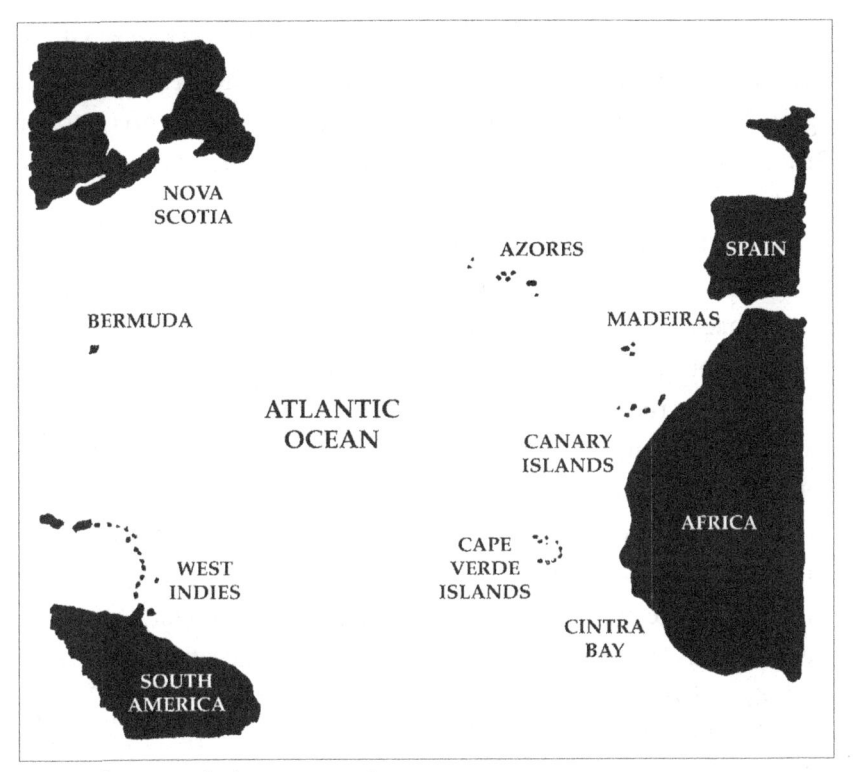

The Atlantic Whaling Grounds.

Provincetown bark *Frank Bunchina* at anchor in Horta harbor. She was able to get some mail from home that had come on the *Bunchina* before going ashore and taking a room at Silva's Hotel. She was further pleased to find that four other captains had their families in the hotel and there was the chance to meet and talk with other females while the boys played with some of their children. The only discordant note that she recorded during these first days ashore was that she had trouble sleeping because of bugs. The hotel beds were full of fleas.

A few days later Clara was feeling ill, so much so that her husband decided to let her stay in Horta while the ship went out for a week in search of whales. She stayed in bed for several days at the hotel and when the ship returned on September 29th, she had regained her strength enough to return to her shipboard home. Once at sea again, her recovery was slow but she felt strong enough on October 3rd to attend a social function aboard the *Bunchina* where she wrote of singing and dancing.

During this period it was common for American whaling ships to visit the Azores to recruit additional crewmembers and in some cases, replace ones that for some reason or another hadn't worked out. In the short time away from home, Clara had already recorded the reduction in rating of one of the mates for "not being capable of doing his job," and another case of a sailor who had refused to go aloft in foul weather. Whaling was a dirty and risky business and foreign crews usually supplemented the local sailors in completing the crewlist. In some cases they composed the majority of the crew. Captain Ryder headed for Terciera for some new recruits. During the time ashore there, one of the men that had signed on in Provincetown, William Perkins, jumped ship. Apparently he was no great loss as Clara recorded that "...we were all glad to let him go."

The *N.D. Chase* spent the rest of October at sea, again without success in taking any whales. The fall weather was comfortable and Clara continued her sewing, knitting, and reading. By the 21st, the ship had reached the vicinity of the Canary Islands and the captain made a stop on the uninhabited south side of San Torote island. The children collected shells and the men caught some fish. Clara picked flowers to brighten her cabin. They climbed part way up the side of a 3,000-foot mountain to the edge of the volcanic cinder cone and took in the view before getting back on the ship that evening.

She had a chance to visit Palmas on Grand Canary Island on October 27th. She was not impressed by the palace, noting, "The city did not look as well as I had fancied it did and as for the people, the majority of them are rather a rough savage looking race. But it is a capital place for fruit. But upon the whole I was rather dissatisfied with the place." While anchored in Palmas, another crewmember deserted. Captain Ryder went to the local authorities and asked that they try to find him and return him to the ship. After a short time at sea again, the whaler returned to Palmas on November 6th and the deserter was back on board.

A happy event happened the next day, when at sea again, the *N.D. Chase* encountered the Provincetown schooner *William Martin*. To Clara's delight, the captain had his wife aboard and she was able to entertain the woman in her cabin for much of the afternoon and evening. "I was very glad to see her," Clara wrote. "Although she was a stranger to me but we were soon acquainted and it was past two at night before we retired. I had four letters from home." Her new friend also had a child with her and he and the Ryder boys played all the following day, the families observing Sabbath services together. The two whalers stayed near each other for almost a week and Clara and the children continued their cross deck visits until the morning of the 13th when the *William Martin* was no more to be seen.

Their next anchorage was Cintra Bay on the African coast.[4] This was a rendezvous point for Atlantic whalers where mail and information were exchanged. A number of vessels were already at anchor when the *N.D. Chase* arrived. Clara noted the presence of the American barks *Messenger*, *Huntress*, and the Portuguese brig *Water Witch*. The American ships had women on board and she visited with them. Later that day, the Provincetown brig *Eschol* arrived and when the *William Martin* came to anchor nearby at 6:00 p.m. there were five women present in the bay. Clara's happiness is reflected in her entry on November 20th. "I wish some of our friends at home could look in upon us and see how we enjoy ourselves. I guess they would think that we took some comfort sometimes at sea as well as on the land."

This easy "gamming" opportunity continued for much of the

remainder of the month as the whalers cruised the waters around Cintra Bay and the African coast. They saw a number of whales but were unable to take any although the *Frank Bunchina* did capture a right whale that yielded 130 barrels of oil. With the *N.D. Chase* still "clean" after almost a half year away from home, Clara revealed a bit of melancholy as she wrote on November 29th, "How often do I look back upon the past and see with my mind's eye where I might have enjoyed myself far better than what I have done. And yet I enjoy the present. Although I am deprived of the society of my friends and of the world, yet I am with those whom I hold dearer than anything else on the earth, for my chief treasures are ever near me, and I am almost constantly engaged in looking after their comfort and welfare." With only a handful of letters from Provincetown since June, she wondered about how her friends and relatives at home were faring. "Are our friends all alive and enjoying the blessing of health? Is kind heaven's propitious smile oer them? Or are they bowed down with grief and sorrow? Do they think of the absent and wish their return? I almost wait for an answer but alas I can have none. I must be patient until I can have them answered."

On December 5, 1857, Clara recorded that she had been away from home 180 days. When the Provincetown whaler *Mountain King* arrived on the 9th, her spirits picked up with some long awaited letters from home. "All well and quite good spirits," she wrote.

She was further pleased to see the *William Martin* again two days later and she was able to enjoy the company of Mrs. Martin for almost a week. On December 15th, the lookout called "there she blows," and the *N.D. Chase* took her first whale of the cruise. It proved to be a fairly small one and yielded only forty barrels of oil. Clara recorded the boiling process and her boys' connection to it. "We are still boiling and I begin to experience something of a whaleman's life for everything is daubed with oil and smoke. But luckily, I do not have any of it in my room only as the children go out and in for they both look as if they belonged to the race of wool heads. But by a hard washing with soap and water, they were made to look quite respectable and when they were put to bed at night, they really looked like themselves. Of my own condition I say nothing and as for Stephen, he is as black and greasy as he well can be."

Cruising with the *William Martin*, the *N.D. Chase* continued to see whales but were unable to successfully take any. On one occasion, they harpooned one of the creatures and followed it for ten hours, only to see it throw the lance and escape in the darkness. On another occasion, the *William Martin* lanced and killed a whale only to have it sink before it could be brought along side.

On Christmas Day, the crew of the *N.D. Chase* took no holiday, continuing to search for the elusive whales. Clara reflected in her cabin on her half year away from home and what the day meant to her. "My mind reverts back to the days of my youth," she wrote, "And in fancy I hear the well known voices of my beloved friends as each one tries to be the first wishing me Merry Christmas. I can even see the stockings as they hang in the chimney corner waiting for that mysterious being called Santa Claus to pop down the chimney and fill them with sugar plums and candy." When little Frank asked if Santa would find them in their anchorage off the coast of Africa, Clara told him that she "was of the opinion that Santa Claus never visits the west coast of Africa unless he comes in the shape of an Arab for we see a plenty of them every day and by all their artful means try to get us near the shore but as the old saying is, a burnt child dreads the fire, therefore we dread them enough to keep out of their reach."

The rough weather, and the sand and dust blowing over the ship from the continent, didn't improve the mood of the day. At least Clara could look forward to seeing the *William Martin* close by. The crew got close enough to harpoon another whale but the line parted and the creature took "french leave" and escaped, trailing four irons and one spade and a good bit of line. On December 30th, the *N.D. Chase* anchored near the *William Martin*, the brig *Eschol*, and the recently arrived Provincetown whaler *Varnum H. Hill*. Although she had the company of her friend Mrs. Martin, she was disappointed at having again lost a whale. "The boats went to cruise as usual," she wrote. "But no New Year's present for us today in the shape of a whale."

The *William Martin* sailed for the West Indies on January 4th and Clara busied herself writing letters to people at home. The departure of the *Martin* was an occasion of sadness for Clara as she had grown quite fond of the captain's wife and her small boy. The *N.D. Chase* parted her anchor line that night and because of the rough weather they had to stay under sail for several days until it cleared enough for the crew to retrieve the buoyed chain. The arrival of the bark *Rothschild* didn't bring any better news as her captain reported that he had been out almost a full year and had only managed twenty-five barrels of sperm oil and little else. They spoke the *Varnum H. Hill* and her captain reported that he had also been unable to take any whales since that ship's arrival on the coast several months previous. Hoping to improve their odds, Captain Ryder agreed to temporarily "mate" with the *Rothschild* and share any whales taken. But, other than a few small Orca whales, the *N.D. Chase* continued her fruitless search of the ocean for oil.

On January 17, 1858, as the *N.D. Chase* cruised through a calm sea, a large right whale was spotted. The starboard boats were lowered and within an hour the crew had killed the creature. After some difficulty trying to keep the whale afloat, they were able to bring her alongside where for the next three days the cutting and boiling process took place. The *Eschol* and *Varnum H. Hill* anchored nearby and offered some assistance in processing the whale. It seemed such a novelty that one of the ships had finally taken a whale in this season of scarcity that other crews came by just to have a look at it. The schooner *Watchman* also joined the three whalers and the captains enjoyed an evening together. Captain Joseph Tuck of the *Frank Bunchina* sent Clara some oranges and some figs and nuts for the children. He invited the family aboard the *Bunchina* and then brought some of his crew over to the *N.D. Chase* where they performed a musical entertainment. The *Chase* cruised with the *Bunchina* until February 3rd, when they anchored once again in Cintra Bay.

Captain Ryder had been ashore in this port several times in earlier cruises. Two years previous, he had gotten into an argument with an Arab there and had ended up shooting the man to death. This time he made it a point to retrieve the skull of the dead native, and presented it to Clara as a souvenir. She referred to this bizarre treasure as a "curiosity," but made no other mention of the unusual circumstances of its origin. They toasted the grotesque treasure aboard the *Bunchina* at a roast pig dinner later that evening.

Captain Ryder pulled one of Clara's infected teeth on February 9th. They cruised for the next week off the African coast in the company of the *Bunchina* and the schooner *Watchman*, spending evenings anchored together and being entertained by the *Bunchina*'s small orchestra. A rat that had been captured aboard the *Bunchina* provided amusement for the children. For the rest of the month the whales proved "shy" and as Clara put it, [they] "seem to think it is not very good fun to be killed." Competition for whales was keen and none of the vessels had agreed to be "mated." At one time the *N.D. Chase* and the bark *Huntress* both harpooned the same whale, but because the *Huntress* had its lance in first, that ship was able to claim it. Several times the crew made fast to a whale only to see the creature throw the barb and escape. Clara blamed the incompetence of the boatsteerers for losing several whales.

On March 2, 1858, the *N.D. Chase* had its third whale, a fairly small one that yielded fifty barrels. Clara was close enough to see the struggle of the creature and showed some sympathy for its fate. "She was within a short distance of the ship all the time they were killing her," she wrote. "I could see every maneuver and hear what was said in the boats. It seemed to me to be almost a pity to kill so noble a creature, one that will struggle so hard and long for dear life. But man, the weakest of God's creatures, overpowers all other animals no matter how great and powerful. And yet how necessary to the comforts of man is the whale. The words of the poet are,

> 'Ho, whales, that sail the briny deep.
> Repine not at your fate.—
> Your flesh illuminates the world
> Your bones, make women, great.'"

Other than a single small killer whale, the rest of March yielded nothing. Clara was concerned about little Frank who took sick on the 24th. "I think he is troubled with worms and has some cold," she recorded. By the end of the month the child's sickness had passed. The *N.D. Chase* shaped a course for the Canary Islands on the first of April to augment the crew with new recruits. On April 3rd,. On April 3rd, they spoke the British ship *Mallard* which was bound for Calcutta. Clara noted that there were two lady passengers on board and she found the potatoes and newspapers that were exchanged "very acceptable." They anchored at Palmas on Grand Canary Island on April 11th where they spent almost two weeks of liberty while the crew reprovisioned the ship.

The stop at Palmas was a much more pleasant break than it had been in the fall. Clara and the boys rode donkeys around the city and enjoyed the verdant gardens and parks. The addition of fresh fruit to the diet was appreciated by all and Clara wrote that she was "feeling in much better spirits than before I went on shore." The *N.D. Chase* weighed anchor on April 20th and headed once again for the African coast and Cintra Bay.

Almost immediately they were into schools of whales and were fortunate to take three of them on April 23rd. After boiling for three days they stowed another two hundred barrels in the hold of the *N.D. Chase*. Clara recorded that the ship now held about 325 barrels of oil and four thousand pounds of bone. They arrived back at Cintra Bay on May 3rd and commenced cleaning and painting the ship. Clara's activities centered around the children and sewing clothing for her husband.

In late May, Clara had the opportunity to go ashore in Cintra Bay where she observed the local population there. As with most encounters with native people by nineteenth century Americans, Clara's journal revealed her low opinion of them. She described them as "...a black, large, savage looking race with their heads shaved close on the sides with a strip of long hair on the middle, which they braid and then fasten on shells, buttons, and every fanciful thing they can get and let it hang down on each side of their head. They live on raw fish, and their clothing is the skins of animals which they kill." Her entry is not unlike the prejudices expressed by most American women of that period who were exposed to cultures that were so different from their own.

The three whales taken in early May proved to be the last ones brought aboard in the Atlantic phase of the cruise. They saw several others but were unable to make fast to any of them. The monotony of fruitless cruising began to weigh on everyone aboard the whaler. "I am quite anxious for something to cause an excitement," Clara wrote on June 8, 1858. But there were no more whales willing to give up their oil for the crew of the *N.D. Chase*.

Arriving again in the Azores, the ship anchored at Horta Harbor in Fayal on June 13th. Clara and the children again took rooms at Silva's Hotel. There were letters from home that had been left for them by other Provincetown ships. Knowing that the *N.D. Chase* was headed on the second long leg of her voyage – this time around Africa and into the Indian Ocean – Clara busied herself in writing

Frank Bunchina Ryder as a young man. This photo was taken months before his death at sea. Courtesy of Mrs. Ralph Manning.

letters that would be sent home before they left. As they departed on June 16th, she couldn't help but think of her friends and family back on Cape Cod and she wondered what they might be doing.

Cruising on a southwesterly course down the African coast, the *N.D. Chase* encountered several ships, which provided a bit of a break in the otherwise dull routine. On July 2nd, they spoke a New Bedford whaler, *Sea Gull*, and were able to get some two-month old newspapers and Clara visited with the captain's wife. Two days later, another New Bedford whaler, the *Henry Kneeland*, was in view and Captain Ryder took the boys on board where they received some fruitcake, jelly, and corn meal and molasses. On the 7th, the Provincetown brig *Panama* hove into view and they were able to get some recent Cape newspapers. Another Provincetown bark, the *Spartan*, sailed near enough on the 9th for them to receive mail and a cake that had been sent from home.

The journal for the remainder of the voyage has been lost. We do know that a month later, on August 12, 1858, Clara gave birth to a baby boy who was named Stephen Morse Ryder. There had been no prior mention of her condition in the journal. The occasional sickness that she recorded the previous fall in the Azores was probably related to the early stages of her pregnancy. The voyage of the *N.D. Chase* continued for the remainder of 1858 and into 1859. The ship returned to Provincetown on October 13, 1859. It was the last whaling voyage for Clara and it proved to be the last for some time for her husband. Captain Ryder volunteered for naval duty during the Civil War and was in service with a couple of breaks from 1861-1865. He was involved in the battle of Mobile Bay under Union Admiral David Farragut and served with distinction until the war's conclusion. He held command of several Provincetown schooners after the war, including the *Allegro*, the *Joseph Lindsey*, and the *Alexander*. While in command of the schooner *Bonnie Eloise*, Stephen A. Ryder died December 27, 1882, in Bocas del Toro in Panama under suspicious circumstances. His death was listed as a result of "bilious fever," but family lore says that there is some evidence that he was poisoned. He was fifty-three years old.

Clara had died the year before in Provincetown on April 2, 1881, at the age of fifty-one. The son she called "Bunny," Frank Bunchina Ryder, grew up and went to sea like his father. He was lost overboard off the Grand Banks on May 4, 1876. He was twenty years old at the time of his death.[5]

• • •

Chapter VIII

"Sewing helps to dispel the monotony that will manifest itself assertively at times."

VIOLA FISH COOK OF PROVINCETOWN

This was an understated remark made by the wife of Captain John Atkins Cook of Provincetown as she talked to a *Boston Globe* reporter about spending the winter of 1901 huddled in her frozen ship's cabin 160 miles north of the Arctic Circle. "One would suppose the voyager would need to hug the fire to avoid perishing when I tell you that the temperature was as low as 57 below zero, and for weeks never rose above 50 during our winter at Baille Island."[1] She was recounting her sixth "wintering over" in the ice-bound Beaufort Sea where for a whole year there hadn't been another white woman within a thousand miles.

Some have referred to Viola Cook as the tragic victim of a relentless Arctic winter where she was driven mad by isolation and her husband's almost maniacal quest to fill his ship with whale oil and bone. Years after her final experience in the Arctic, people in Provincetown remembered her as a crazy old lady who cursed like a sailor and talked to herself as she walked along Commercial Street. There were some who whispered of hearing strange singing coming from her house in the middle of the night and of her

Viola Cook in the Arctic. Courtesy of Cape Cod Community College.

reported habit of constantly sharpening long kitchen knives during the day. Eugene O'Neil cast a thinly disguised character based on Viola in his 1917 play *Ile*. His portrayal had her playing the piano wildly in the darkened cabin of her frozen whaleship, her mind disintegrating while her Ahab-like husband blindly pursued his ghostly whales.

It certainly hadn't started out this way for Viola Delphine Fish of Hyannis. Born in 1855 to Silas and Mary Fish, she was married at the age of twenty-two to John Atkins Cook of Provincetown, a man who was several years her junior. By the mid-1880's, he had risen to become one of the Cape tip's most noted whaling captains. A blatant self-promoter, Captain Cook billed himself as the "King of the Deep" and his ego most certainly equalled the size of the creatures that he pursued at sea. Eventually, he became part of a handful of whalers who worked the treacherous waters of the Beaufort Sea between Point Barrow, Alaska and the Admundsen Gulf off Arctic Canada. Generally, the weather in this area was condusive to whaling only from mid-June through mid-September – a very short time to exploit the valuable bowhead whale population that lived there. The Beaufort Sea had only been explored and mapped in the late 1880's and was relatively unknown to east coast whalers.

Viola Cook made her first voyage to the western Arctic in 1893 aboard the steam bark *Narvarch*. She was excited to visit the region and gave no indication that she had any misgivings about the prospect of spending the winter in the high latitudes. On this particular trip there were other American whalers working the grounds between Herschel Island and Cape Bathurst and they had their wives with them. Like the other captains in the mix, Captain Cook planned to "winter over" in the shelter of Pauline Cove at Herschel Island, which was west of the Mackenzie River at about the seventieth degree of northern latitude. This would allow the whalers to be in position in the spring to move directly to the

Captain John Atkins Cook. Courtesy of Cape Cod Community College.

business of whaling as the ice broke up in June. The wintering over procedure involved anchoring the ship in line with the prevailing wind and allowing it to become frozen in and covered with a heavy pack of insulating snow. The steam boiler aboard the *Narvarch* was fed with tons of driftwood that the crew gathered and cut before the darkness of winter set in. This made the ship essentially a wooden igloo, snug against the 20-40 below zero winter temperatures that prevailed there.

During this first winter, Viola had the company of four other women at Pauline Cove. The *Jesse Freeman*, *Beluga*, *Thrasher*, and the *Alexander* joined the *Narvarch* at the anchorage. It was, for the most part, a pleasant, almost gay experience for her. The women staged elaborate dinners and played whist. In a communal building on shore there were parties and activities for the small contingent of whaling families. But still, there were forced periods of inactivity due to the weather and in the spring of 1894 Viola told her husband that she would like to return to Provincetown at the end of the short summer. But, in what would later become a familiar pattern, Captain Cook told her that the ship hadn't taken enough oil and that they would be staying another winter. That winter turned into a third and the *Narvarch* didn't return to San Francisco until November of 1896.[2]

From his point of view, Captain Cook thought Viola was having a splendid time. In his accounts he talked of skating parties, sledding, musical recitals, and hunting trips. For him, this was an adventure that featured dancing, billiard playing in the storehouse on shore, and "an almost unending round of festivities." The cold and darkness appear to have been only a minor inconvenience for Captain Cook. "Outside at such times there might be noted the swish and swirl of frozen snow granules," he wrote in a later memoir. "The bitter biting breath of a temperature half a hundred degrees below zero and Stygian darkness, or the twilight – that uncanny half-darkness, found only in high latitudes and which prevails for weeks at a time at certain seasons of the year. Within walls, however, men and women, hedged by bunting decorations and bathed in the glare of swinging deck-lanterns, danced merrily. As the heat from the many wood stoves combined with the unwonted exercise set the blood coursing madly through the reveler's veins, coats and vests of fur and skin would be flung aside and the owners danced in shirt-waists and well-worn flannel."[3]

After a year ashore in Provincetown, during which Captain Cook negotiated the purchase of a new vessel, the former Norwegian whaler *Haardraade*, Viola was able to reacquaint herself with her only daughter, Emma. It was decided that the teenaged Emma should accompany her mother and father to Sweden where the new vessel, now renamed *Bowhead*, would be picked up. Since the girl had just graduated from high school, it seemed the perfect time to have her experience traveling the world in a ship. In the spring of 1898, they took a steamer from New York to London and then a second steamer to Sweden to board the 500-ton steam bark. In a voyage that was a pleasure for Viola and certainly must have served as an education for Emma, Captain Cook plotted a course through the Mediterranean Sea and the Suez Canal and into the Indian Ocean. At Yokohama, Japan, the *Bowhead* was refitted for Arctic whaling and in the spring of 1899 they sailed into the Bering Strait and around Point Barrow into the Beaufort Sea.

Having her daughter aboard on this cruise seemed to make all the difference for Viola. The two women enjoyed visiting foreign ports along their route and the winter of 1899-1900 allowed mother and daughter to develop a closer relationship despite the difficulties of living in such a harsh environment. There was a piano on board and Emma was an accomplished player. The young girl entertained the crews and families that were sharing the "wintering over" experience. But there were problems with the crew and Captain Cook's harsh methods of rendering discipline almost led to a mutiny on the *Bowhead*. In this increasingly tense

The steam bark Bowhead. *Courtesy of Cape Cod Community College.*

atmosphere, the ship left the Beaufort Sea and returned to San Francisco in the fall of the year 1900.

Viola went north again in the spring of 1901, without Emma, and spent an isolated winter anchored at Baille Island, a remote site almost two hundred miles west of Herschel Island. During that winter she endured a fifty-eight day spell of unbroken darkness huddled in her cabin. She was the only woman in the small fleet of whalers anchored there and found her isolation further deepened by the absense of other females. Despite the fact that the voyage had been a good money maker for her husband – one account has the ship making $115,000[4] – Viola told her husband that she would not return to the Arctic again. She announced in the summer of 1902 that she would no more endure life aboard a whaler. Captain Cook, not a man used to any sort of objections to his plans, was

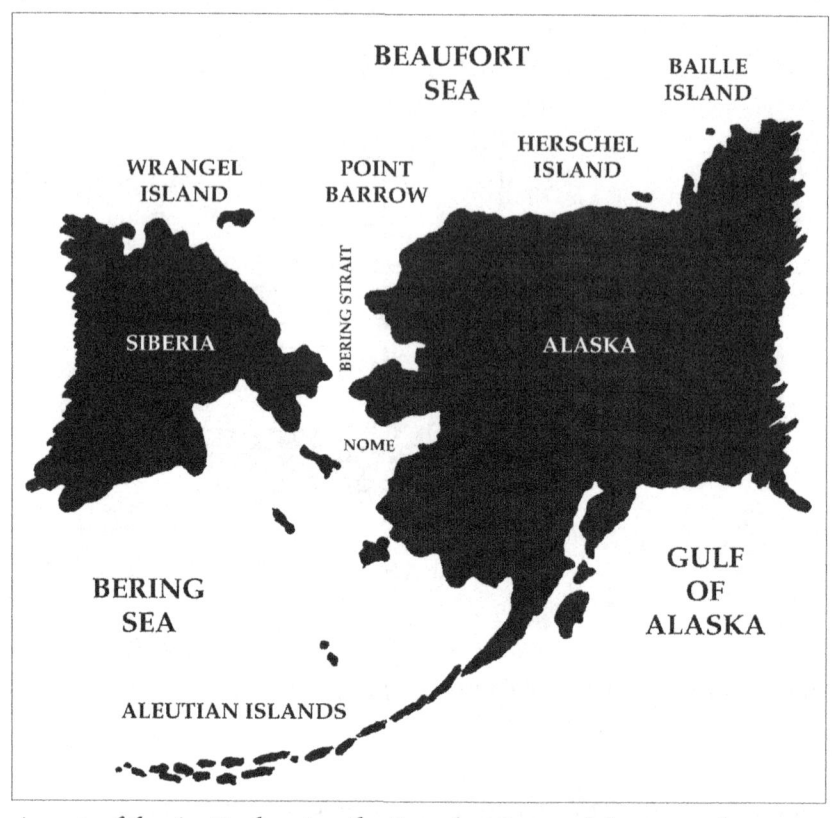

A map of the Arctic showing the Beaufort Sea and the normal extent of open water along the Canadian and Alaskan northern coast during July and August. Herschel Island and Baille Island were the two main anchorages for the few Arctic whale ships that chose to "winter over" in this harsh environment. The fact that the ice never really broke up enough to allow a passage back around Point Barrow was the reason that Viola Cook had to spend an extra year of 1905-1906. She was never the same after her experience in that frozen world.

very upset. He left Provincetown alone by rail for San Francisco in the spring of the following year.

For some reason, either guilt, obligation, or perhaps out of fear of her husband's temperament, Viola had a change of heart and wired her husband that she would meet him in Nome, Alaska later

The Bowhead *in heavy Arctic ice. Courtesy of Cape Cod Community College.*

that spring. She rendezvoused with him there on June 20, 1903. Captain Cook told her that they would only be staying for the summer and would return to San Francisco that fall. But during July and August, they took only a single whale and when the time for returning came, Captain Cook, without consulting his wife, headed for the old anchorage at Herschel Island. That winter Viola was again the only white woman in the Arctic. The summer of 1904 proved no better for the taking of whales and with only four added to the single creature from the year before, Captain Cook decided that another winter in the ice was necessary. Faced with a restless crew and a diminished food and fuel supply, the captain stubbornly continued his obsessive Arctic odyssey into the summer of 1905. Viola begged him to bring the *Bowhead* back to San Francisco before the ice closed in again. She told him she would rather die than spend another season locked in the cold and icy darkness. But this time it was nature that thwarted Viola's plans. As the *Bowhead* attempted to sail west toward Point Barrow, the ice shifted and blocked their path. By September, Captain Cook had no choice but to bring his ship back to the protected anchorage at Herschel Island. With three other whale ships, the *Beluga*, *Herman*, and *Narwhal*, and the later arriving *Belvedere*, the *Bowhead* set herseelf up for another long winter in the ice. There were no women aboard any of these ships.

Even Captain Cook now realized that the relentless Arctic winters and the loneliness that had consumed his wife over the previous two seasons had pushed her to the edge. "Her contentment and vivacity fled, giving place to despondency. And she became even more serious affected as the days passed," he reflected some years later..."The disappointment fairly overwhelmed her. So completely was she prostrated by grief, her nervous system was shattered and she eventually sank in melancholia – a state from which she did not recover until she had been more than a year in her own home and even then not fully."[5]

In addition to coming down with scurvy in that ninth winter in the ice, Viola also witnessed the increasing brutality of her husband as he tried to maintain order and discipline in a crew that had long since stopped following his orders. Faced with mutiny, Captain Cook resorted to physical punishment and had several of the crew members locked below for extended periods. Viola could not have helped but be affected by what she saw and heard outside her cabin door. When the ship finally returned to San Francisco in the summer of 1906, she was a broken woman.[6]

Vowing never to again set foot on a whaling vessel, Viola nevertheless was coaxed back to sea in 1910 at age fifty-five aboard a new 200-ton brig that her husband had built in Essex, Massachusetts. It carried the name *Viola* and apparently that honor was enough to entice her to leave Provincetown once again. The ship was headed for an eighteen-month voyage for Atlantic sperm whales, but less than six months out Viola developed beriberi

The whaler Viola. *Courtesy of Cape Cod Community College.*

and had to be put off at St. Helena and brought back home by steamship. It was her final voyage.

Viola Cook's last years were tragic. Never fully recovered from what clearly was a case of severe depression, she became an object of gossip in her home town. Her husband was frequently away on voyages. One writer made the observation that when he was home, Captain Cook was afraid to sleep in his room without a heavy dresser pushed against the door for fear that Viola might kill him with one of the kitchen knives that she was constantly honing.[7]

Perhaps mercifully, Viola Cook died of heart failure on November 20, 1922. She had been an invalid for some years before her death. Her passing came just six days before Captain Cook completed the final paperwork on his divorce from her so he could be declared legally married to Ethel Sparks, the widow of his friend Captain Frederick Sparks. Captain Cook was sixty-five. His new bride was thirty-eight. He had married his new wife without even waiting for his divorce from Viola to be final. The marriage scandalized Provincetown, most of the residents feeling that Captain Cook was a scoundrel who was abandoning a sick and faithful wife for a younger woman. The captain lost his seat on the Provincetown Board of Trade and was kicked out of the local Masonic Lodge. He was threatened with tar and feathers if he were ever to return to the Cape tip and there is no evidence that he ever did. Moving to Florida where he went into the citrus fruit business, Captain Cook died in July of 1938 in Coral Gables, Florida, where he is buried. His wife Viola, who had been, in the account of one local newspaper, "tossed aside in her declining years," rests in the Gifford cemetery in Provincetown.

Daughter Emma, the only child of John and Viola Cook, married Frank Knowles Atkins of Provincetown. They had four children. She died in 1945 and is also buried in the Gifford cemetery. As for the brig *Viola*, she was sold to Captain Joseph Luis of Provincetown and disappeared in the Atlantic with all hands in the summer of 1918, possibly the victim of a German submarine.

• • •

Chapter IX

"I think I have learned to bear disappointment bravely."

Didama KelleyDoane of West Harwich

When Didama Kelley married Captain Uriel Doane Jr. of West Harwich on October 17, 1860, she was well aware of the fact that she was entering a life that would require a number of sacrifices. Her twenty-two year old husband, who was her second cousin, would become a respected master mariner whose voyages eventually took him around the world. Didama would accompany him in a sailing career that would measure almost twenty years. When it was over, she had sailed around Cape Horn almost a dozen times and had circumnavigated the globe four times. She had been shipwrecked twice and had seen the loss of her husband's proud clipper ship in the Pacific. Through it all she maintained her dignity and good spirits despite the disappointments that often plagued her shipboard life.

The fact that her husband was actually a fairly close relative was not that unusual on Cape Cod in the mid-nineteenth century. Usually a few families dominated the villages and the opportunity for marriage to an outsider was rare. In Harwich there was a close association of Nickersons, Doanes, Kelleys, and Chases and in

Didama Kelley Doane. Courtesy of Syracuse University Press.

most marriages there were already established family ties. As the daughter of Isaiah Kelley, Didama knew all of these families and when the chance presented itself to formally be joined with one of them, it was a given that this was the way it should be.

Didama's voyages around the world were brought to light in the publication of a 1946 book by one of her grand nephews. Her first voyage and her final one are the subject of this sketch and it is *The Cap'n's Wife*, by Albert Joseph George, that provides the bulk of the narrative. All quotes are from that work, which was published by Syracuse University Press.

After six years of marriage, Didama Kelley Doane was eager to spend more time with her husband. She hadn't seen much of him since their wedding day. The Civil War had parted the couple frequently because Captain Doane felt that the threat of Confederate privateers was too much to contemplate bringing Didama aboard ship. Captain Doane made his voyages without the company of his wife during the war years. But in 1866, the conflict had been resolved and from New Orleans, where he was loading cotton aboard his clipper ship *Rival*, Uriel telegraphed his wife that she should join him in that southern port and sail back to Boston with him.

Without hesitation, Didama packed her bags and took the train to New York where she boarded the steamer *George Washington* for the voyage south. On May 19th the steamer passed through the narrows and out past Sandy Hook. This was Didama's first trip away from her Harwich home and she found the initial experience exhilarating. Calm seas and steady progress in the week-long voyage to New Orleans no doubt lulled her into thinking that the sea life would be comfortable and easy. She had a chance to visit the Mississippi port for several weeks as the *Rival* finished her loading. On July 21, 1866, the ship put to sea and sailed into the Gulf of Mexico. Almost immediately Didama found that life aboard ship was not going to be as easy as she had previously imagined. Sick

Captain Uriel Doane. Courtesy of Syracuse University Press.

from the first day out, she stayed in her cabin as the ship bucked headwinds and rough seas around Florida. On August 3rd, she made her feeling clear about how she viewed the ocean: "...I do wish that the All Powerful One who ruleth the winds and waves and who holdeth the waters in the hollow of His hand will see fit to change the wind and give us prosperous breezes and I doubt not He will do so in His own good time. It is for us to bow in submission to His will."[1]

The trip up the coast, while rough, was fairly quick and on August 12, 1866 they sighted the "three sisters" lighthouses of Nauset and were into Boston Harbor the next day. Didama took the train back to Harwich where she stayed with her family while Captain Doane concluded his business in Boston. Three weeks later, she got a telegram from her husband instructing her to meet him in New York to begin a voyage that would take them out to California and San Francisco.

Fortunately, regular train service had been established into Harwich the year earlier and Didama made an easy connection from the little North Harwich depot to the main line into New York. With hardly a day for her to look at that city, *Rival* weighed anchor and headed to Philadelphia to load 1,400 tons of coal for delivery in San Francisco. There, Didama had several weeks to prepare for the long voyage and stayed at the Arch Street House where the wives of sea captains lived ashore. The *Rival* was tied up at the big coal pier in Chester, Pennsylvania. On September 17, 1866, the ship headed down the Delaware River and the beginning of the long voyage out to the west coast.

Fall can be a difficult time on the east coast for sailors. Tropical depressions create weather conditions that test even the best of ships and men. For Didama, the rolling sea kept her confined to her bed and the constant rolling motion of the ship made her very sick. Even the captain and crew were affected by the heavy seas and the ship labored to make progress against the wind. On September

26th, Didama noted that the captain and the third mate were sick and recorded that the ship had lost two topsails to the gale. The wind didn't moderate for another two weeks and it took forty days to reach the equator. They were sailing with the New York clipper *Chieftain* and Didama fretted that they needed the help of the almighty to guarantee the sailing reputation of Cape Cod against the competitor.

The rough passage toward Cape Horn was accompanied by fog and poor visibility. Captain Doane often had to rely on dead reckoning, being unable to take a good sun angle to fix the *Rival*'s position. All this time Didama struggled to maintain something of a normal routine in her shipboard home. On November 23rd, she congratulated herself on her accomplishments. "Have made two bleached chemises for myself, one calico dress, one bleached cloth shirt, with eleven tucks, two undershirts for Uriel and six bleached cloth shirts, made and stitched the wristbands, besides mending. Think I have done pretty well."[2]

The journal entries for late-November and into mid-December reflect Didama's concerns for the approaching run around the Horn. With the constant headwinds and the need to proceed carefully without good navigation marks, it was almost ninety days out of Philadelphia before the *Rival* was even in the vicinity of this southern-most piece of South America. Once there, they took another three weeks to make the turn around the Horn. Several other vessels also found it quite an ordeal to make it past this final hurdle into the Pacific. Another Cape Cod woman, Mary Knowles of Brewster, was aboard her husband's clipper *White Swallow* in that same season and attested to the difficulty of the passage by noting in her journal, "You ought to see the track on the chart. It looks as if a hen had been walking over a little space."[3] On January 5, 1867, Didama wrote, "I can truly say I have no particular desire ever to come the same voyage again... We are all well, which is a great blessing. Pigs all dead. About twenty-four days getting

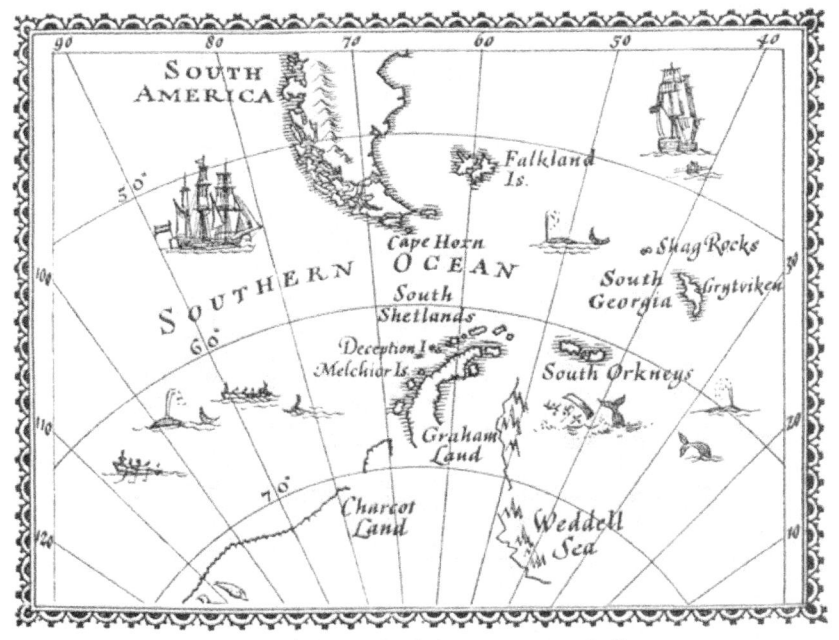

Cape Horn. Courtesy of Cape Cod Community College.

around Cape Horn."[4] But this was only the beginning of Didama's troubles. Fresh water was in short supply and the specter of scurvy was becoming a real issue.

For some reason, Captain Doane chose not to stop at one of the Chilean or Peruvian ports on the west coast of South America. While rain in early February alleviated some of the fresh water shortage, the poor diet on board furthered the problem of scurvy. Didama noted that two of the crew had advanced cases of the disease. "Sam has been sick about a week," she wrote. "I'm afraid the other is a hopeless case. His gums are spongy and his teeth loose. Our flour is most out, our bread most gone and O dear me."[5]

On March 2, 1867, the *Rival* was finally off San Francisco and a pilot came on board to bring the ship into an anchorage at Mare Island. The voyage had taken almost six months. The sick crewmen were taken off and Uriel and Didama established a temporary

The golden age of sail was typified by the clipper ship. Perhaps the ultimate accomplishment of maritime architecture, these vessels were in their prime from the late 1840s until the age of steam brought an end to their dominance in the 1870s.

residence in Vallejo from which they could take in the sights of the golden city. Didama caught up on mail from home and the national news. Daily excursions around San Francisco delighted her. But in late-March, Uriel told his wife that they were not going to be headed back home just yet. The *Rival* had orders to take a cargo of freight to Hawaii and then would proceed to Bakers Island with a number of native laborers to load guano for shipment to Europe. During the almost two-week voyage to Hawaii, Didama made no log entries but continued with her sewing and reading.

Hawaii made a favorable impression on Didama and she was able to spend a week there in the company of Mrs. Ethelinda Lewis of Martha's Vineyard, whose husband's whaler *Corinthian* was laying in supplies for a trip to the Arctic. The two women shopped and visited the lush gardens around the royal family's residence. But the time in port passed all too quickly and on April 17th the anchor was pulled and *Rival* set sail for Bakers Island.[6]

This was a period in history when there was a great demand for natural fertilizer – particularly in Europe where years of poor agricultural use had robbed the soil of nutrients. A thriving trade in nitrogen-rich bird droppings motivated many ship owners to send vessels to the Pacific Islands where an almost inexhaustible source of manure was found on a number of remote atolls. The odorous product was mined by indentured Chinese labor and shipped in American ship hulls.

While *Rival* was being loaded with guano, Didama spent most of the days in her cabin. There was no opportunity to go ashore because there was no town to visit. Perhaps because she had more time for reflection, she confided in her journal that she was growing tired of the sea and her isolation from other women. In this melancholy state she passed her 28th birthday on May 8, 1867. "This is my birthday and it has been spent very unpleasantly. Had a crying spell before breakfast and have felt like crying all day. Hope it is no bad omen. How can a person help their feelings? I believe I am twenty-eight years old. Twenty-eight years old! Is it possible!"[7]

When the ship sailed at the end of May, Didama faced not only the uncertainty of where *Rival* would ultimately unload her cargo in Europe, but she also knew that the way to the continent was blocked by Cape Horn. She thought about that "dreaded place" and the bad weather that marked it on their initial passage and didn't make another journal entry until late-June when the ship neared the western approach to the Horn. As she had feared, the seas were heavy and conditions difficult. *Rival* rolled badly and, as she and Uriel sat down to dinner one night, the table broke loose from its fastenings, flinging silverware, dishes, and the drinking glasses across the cabin. She got little sleep and kept little food down before the ship successfully navigated the Horn by the end of June.

Once into the Atlantic, the weather cleared and the winds became more favorable. *Rival* was making as much as 200 miles a day, far more than the average of 35-50 that had been covered on the leg into San Francisco. Other than one incident of two crewmen fighting over some issue, for which the captain put them in irons for a short period, the cruise across the Atlantic to Kinsale, Ireland was quite pleasant. They had been out from Bakers Island for 102 days.

Now almost one full year away from her home, Didama had become a veteran seafarer. She accepted the rigors of life on the ocean as the price she was paying to accompany her husband. But it was clear that, had she the power to direct *Rival* to her next port, that destination would have been Boston and home. Twelve months of living without the amenities that most landbound people took for granted were starting to erode her enthusiasm for the seagoing life. *Rival* was directed to drop the guano cargo in Hamburg, Germany where, at last, Didama could take leave of her small cabin and luxuriate in the wide suite of rooms at the Elbe Hotel. But her comfort was shortlived when her husband told her that their next port was not going to be Boston, but rather, Calcutta, India – half a world away and many months at sea. When *Rival* left Hamburg on her way across the North Sea to load coal in late-October, Didama wrote candidly about the long voyage ahead. "I am sick of going to sea, wind blowing a gale about all the time, ahead of that. Who wouldn't be tired of the seas?"[8]

The trip to India was monotonous, and as the ship neared the equator, very hot. Storms did some minor damage to the vessel, but nothing serious. Christmas and New Year's passed without much celebration and *Rival* was occasionally becalmed on a glassy sea. Where Didama had earlier dreaded the cold of the Cape Horn passage, she now suffered the oppressive heat of the summer latitudes as they approached the Cape of Good Hope. After six months, *Rival* arrived in Calcutta where Didama learned that the ship's agents had scheduled the return voyage to New York. After being away from home for more than a year and a half, this was welcome news. Didama had about a month to see the Indian port city and she filled her cabin with souvenirs for her Cape Cod friends and family.

The final leg of Didama Kelley Doane's sea odyssey saw *Rival* leaving Calcutta in late-May of 1867. Her journal is filled with questions about how members of her family had fared during her absence. That her longing for home was real and genuine can be easily gathered from her log entries. Each day of calm, or of headwinds, seemed like a barrier between Didama and her Cape Cod relatives. The voyage home seemed interminable.

In July, a young crewmember was lost overboard in rough weather near the Cape of Good Hope. Maritime historians know that when this happened, the captain would note the loss with brief remarks. Latitude/longitude positions, the name of the individual, and his rank, if he had one, would be entered in the log. Not much more could be expected of captains who were hardened to what the sea could bring. But for women, such an occurrence brought out genuine feelings of sadness and loss. Didama's remarks about how the sailor was lost are detailed and moving. Her evaluation of how the news would be received by his family was even more poignant. "In a few minutes after the sudden catastrophe the sun came up shining so brightly into our cabin, but not on him who only less than one short hour was with his comrades. So quick that only 'a splash and a dash and the scene over.' And the waves rolled on as they rolled before. During the day had his chest brought aft and examined. There were photographs of boyish-looking faces resembling him, showing that somewhere there is a group of anxious ones awaiting his return which, alas, will be no more on earth."[9]

At this point, Didama's dedication to keeping a daily journal seems to have flagged. Only two more entries were made as the ship crossed the Atlantic to New York. With the prospect of seeing loved ones again, the long leg from the west African coast seemed to take forever. About 1,000 miles from New York the food began to give out and the crew were put on short rations. But the closeness of the final port may have mitigated the shortcomings of what was in the ship's galley and we hear no complaints from Didama. By Thanksgiving, she had arrived home in West Harwich, having spent more than two years aboard her seagoing home and having traveled over 50,000 nautical miles![10]

One would think that this long experience at sea would have been enough for anyone, especially a small frail woman who missed her mother. But Didama Kelley Doane subsequently went back to sea a number of times with her husband, eventually rounding that "dreaded Cape Horn" eleven more times. In 1874, Captain Doane took command of the new 1,500-ton clipper *Granger*, which made regular runs between Liverpool and San Francisco as part of the California/European grain trade. On one of the voyages, the ship's orders were changed to take a coal cargo to Manila in the Philippines. In late October of 1877, the vessel piled onto Swallow Rock Shoal in the Indian Ocean. Despite the efforts of her crew, *Granger* became a total loss. Didama was aboard and had to evacuate the wreck, taking to a small boat in the teeth of a raging gale. Because they were outside of the regular shipping lanes, Captain Doane made plans to try to sail to Singapore, which was more than 800 miles away. Fortunately, after just a few days, the survivors were picked up by the Hong Kong-bound French bark *Sainte Adresse*. This time, when the couple returned home to West Harwich, Uriel Doane "swallowed the anchor" and became a landsman. His wife did not complain about the end of her days and years at sea. As a retired mariner, Captain Doane continued to be active in town affairs, serving a three-year term as a Harwich

Selectman. He was elected a member of the Boston Marine Society in 1878 and died in January of 1897, at the age of fifty-nine. Didama outlived her husband by almost thirty years, passing away in May of 1926. They rest forever together in the Pine Grove Cemetery in West Harwich.

• • •

Chapter X

"My Poor Wifey is Dead and Gone"

BETHIA KNOWLES MAYO SEARS OF BREWSTER

Not every sea experience by women had a happy ending. Bethia Knowles Mayo Sears, the nineteen-year old wife of Captain Elisha Freeman Sears of Brewster, sailed from Boston in October of 1855 on a voyage to San Francisco and the Far East. It was her first sea experience. Less than a year later she was dead, probably a victim of some disease picked up in Calcutta. The loss of his young bride devastated the twenty-two year old captain. He brought her body back to Cape Cod and to her mother and sisters who had received her letters with such excitement.

Bethia was the daughter of Joseph Knowles Mayo, a farmer from Orleans. She had known Elisha Freeman Sears only a short time before they were married on September 6, 1855. An up and coming sea captain, Elisha had just been placed in command of the two-year old Medford-built 177-foot, 1,044-ton clipper *Wild Ranger*.[1] The voyage out to San Francisco and to India was to be a honeymoon trip for the young couple. As she sat in her cabin in Boston Harbor in early October while the ship was being loaded, Bethia looked at the blank pages of her journal and vowed

Captain Elisha Freeman Sears. Courtesy of Cape Cod Community College.

to be faithful in making entries so that her sisters at home could eventually share in some of her seagoing experiences. It was a vow that she would keep despite constant references to what she called "this uninteresting journal." But on that day it was hard to concentrate on writing. Everything was all so new to her. The bustle of the busy harbor and the noises of the waterfront were far different from the quiet villages she had known on Cape Cod.

The *Wild Ranger* was soon towed down through the harbor islands and set a course for what turned out to be a rather slow 130-day passage to San Francisco. Bethia suffered the usual early bouts with seasickness, but seems to have taken well to her first sea experience, venturing above decks frequently and learning the basics of navigation under Elisha's instruction. His pride in his new bride was evident when, on November 4th, he noted that "wife gets along better than I expected her to. She has not vomited (excuse me) but four times since leaving port and we have had considerable heavy weather." The note was penned into Bethia's journal, undoubtedly because Elisha wanted his wife to see it and know how proud of her he was. Bethia, while learning to "box the compass," began to teach her husband to knit and do embroidery. Her journal, written in neat script, made it clear that she was adapting well to shipboard life. She recorded eating pork and beans for dinner with gooseberry pie for dessert and washing the meals down with spruce beer, and she declared herself to be "leading a lazy life," as the ship worked south toward the equator. The couple had packed along pieces of their wedding cake and shared some with the mates hoping that at least a bit of it might be saved for the celebration of the ship's return to Boston.

The approach of warmer latitudes held discomfort for Bethia as the temperatures rose into the 90's. There are indications that she was a bit on the plump side and she suffered with the heat. "This has been the hottest day we have had," she wrote on October 26th. "Temperature 92 in the shade. Imagine ye who read this,

The Wild Ranger. *Courtesy of the Dennis Historical Society.*

how a person of my size and my flesh must suffer."[2] She got badly sunburned. The *Wild Ranger* strugled to find wind and spent the better part of a week becalmed in occasional rain squalls. Overcast skies made it difficult for Elisha to calculate the ship's exact position and his anxiety at the slow progress of the passage brought on a moodiness that Bethia noted in her journal. The rains meant that the hatches and windows often had to be closed and the aft cabin was hot and stuffy. Finally, in the Southeast Trades, they crossed "the line" on Thursday, November 8th. A few days later Bethia saw the South American coast, her first look at land since leaving Boston. "How good it seemed to see land once more. We went within three or four miles of it and I could distinguish trees, hills, banks, etc. I should have liked much to have gone ashore and taken a ramble over 'Eastern Brazil,' but the water began to grow shoalar [sic.] and we turned and fled from it as if something horrible."[3]

As the *Wild Ranger* closed on its passage around Cape Horn, it grew colder and Bethia noted that she had taken her woolens out of storage. Her main physical trouble at this point was a painful toothache. "I am sorry that I did not follow my mother's advice and have it extracted when in Boston," she wrote on November 21st. "Elisha says the steward has a good pair of pincers and that he will pull it for me." She confronted a large rat in her cabin the next day and her screams brought the mate down the hatchway and he pelted the creature with a shoe. "But he finally disappeared behind the setee. And he has not been heard of since. After this excitement I sought my resting place."[4]

Elisha and Bethia finished the last of their wedding cake on Thanksgiving day. The pastry had started to mold and needed to be eaten. Plans of having the last bite on their arrival day back in Boston were finished. While Bethia missed her family on this special day, she wrote that she had "never enjoyed a Thanksgiving better in my life."

Cape Horn weather was always unpredictable but most mariners' references to it used the term "dreaded place." Nearing the Strait of Magellan, the *Wild Ranger* ran into gale winds and heavy seas. Bethia described the weather as being some of the worst she had seen so far. But she had developed her sea legs every bit as much as the rest of the crew and she marveled at the violence of nature. "The clouds hanging in black heavy masses around looking awfully wicked. Large hail stones flying about skipping everything with great violence. The ship laying over on her side as if never to rise again. The terrible howling of the wind all conspired to render the scene grand yet terrific. Did not feel frightened at all... The sailors have the worst of it and I pity them."[5]

On December 11, 1855, the ship completed its westward passage around Cape Horn. The weather gods had been kind to the *Wild Ranger* and, even with a "head sea," the ship began to move slowly north along the west coast of South America. A small stove had been installed in the aft cabin and, though it tended to smoke in certain winds, Bethia spent most of the day there reading, knitting, and making occasional batches of molasses candy for Elisha.

Fresh water availability became a problem as the *Wild Ranger* worked its way north across the equator again. Elisha put the men on water rations. The crew didn't like it and complained. Bethia played the role she was supposed to and took her husband's side. "Elisha put them on allowance giving them each a gallon a day and that is certainly enough for anyone to drink. They love to grumble about something. Shall be glad when we get in port to get rid of the nuisances."[6] Continuing head winds put a gloomy pall over the captain and Bethia noted his continual fretting about his "hard luck" in such slow progress. She prayed for the fair winds that the Trades would bring and her prayers were answered on January 5th. "We now have a seven knot breeze, all sail set and Elisha is quite himself again." Being "himself" allowed Elisha to concentrate on small things below decks. "Elisha has commenced to cure my warts with caustic, it is very painful," Bethia wrote the next day.

On January 22nd, it rained enough so as to improve the conditions for the crew but the winds died and the ship wallowed in the Pacific doldrums. Hardly managing even steerage, the ship recorded days of only 20 to 30 miles of forward progress. Elisha continued to fret, cursing his luck and worrying about the length of his voyage. Less than five hundred miles from San Francisco, the weather turned cold and foggy. It was difficult to plot an accurate position and Elisha came down with a severe cold. Bethia ministered to him by soaking his feet and preparing physics. He recovered but had to spend lengthy periods on deck directing the ship's course in the ever changing winds. It seemed that the *Wild Ranger* would never reach San Francisco.

But on February 14, 1856, the ship was near the Farallon Islands, sounding 42 fathoms, and the next day sailed into San Francisco Harbor. After more than four months at sea, Bethia was excited to regain the stability of solid ground again. "I think I felt nearly as happy as Columbus did on discovering the new continent. They knelt and embraced the earth. I could have done the same."[7]

Mail had been delivered via Panama and there were a number of letters from home to read. Gratefully, Bethia recorded that all was well back on Cape Cod. Elisha, for all his "fretting," was satisfied that his run from Boston was not the slowest of the season. In fact, several clippers that had sailed before the *Wild Ranger* had not arrived yet. Some of the Cape shipmasters that were in San Francisco called to pay respects and to congratulate the young skipper on his voyage.

After less than two weeks in San Francisco, a place that Bethia found to be hard and disagreeable – full of "miserable shacks," the *Wild Ranger* put to sea again, this time bound for Calcutta, India. The brief stay in port did not allow the ship to be thoroughly cleaned up and made shipshape. The aft cabin was in disarray. With the exception of the mates, the ship had an entirely new crew and Bethia had a new steward. "A little dandy – black as soot," she described him. He subsequently proved to have little knowledge of the art of cooking. They were also carrying a passenger that Bethia disapproved of because of the man's drinking and for the fact that he was billeted in the aft cabin area, affecting her privacy. Hardly out a few days, the lightly loaded ship ran into a violent storm and Bethia recorded "paying homage to old Neptune" again while trying to avoid being struck by pieces of furniture that flew around the cabin in the surging seas.

Bad weather continued into March and Bethia wrote frequently of feeling sick and being unable to get out of bed. Her energy level was low and she was feeling the effects of another bad tooth. Passing near the Hawaiian Islands, Bethia wrote of her desire to stop there, but Elisha told her that he could not afford the time off course.

They picked up the trade winds on March 13th and the weather moderated. On March 17th, a frightful event took place as one of

Grave marker of Bethia Sears. Lower Road Cemetery, Brewster. Photo by Jim Coogan.

the sailors fell overboard. "At about eight o'clock last evening, as E & I were in the pantry taking a lunch, we were suddenly startled by the cry of 'Boy Overboard!' E. sprang out of the foreword door, ran for the life buoy, and threw it over close by the head of the boy. As might be expected, there was a great deal of confusion. I ran immediately on deck. The helm was put down as soon as possible. In a very short space of time the boat was launched and put over, the mate with four hands sprang into it and were off in the twinkling of an eye. The shrieks of the boy were plainly heard from the ship which was a guide in finding him. Everything was done that could be done. And we were all watching in anxious suspense for the return of the boat which would be bearer of good or evil tidings. In about ten or fifteen minutes it was seen nearing the ship. E. dreaded almost to inquire for fear they had been unsuccessful. But the response of 'Yes Sir' that greeted our ears relieved our anxious minutes. He had succeeded in reaching the buoy which is all that saved his life as it was said he could not swim. He is 17 years old."[8]

The rescue of the young sailor served as a wonderful present for the day. It was Bethia's 20th birthday – a fact noted by her as "carrying me out of my teens." Her body was apparently serving as a present of sort for fleas that infested the ship. "They bite no one but me and I am nearly devoured." Flies and cockroaches and oppressive heat increased her misery.

Approaching the Singapore Straits, the *Wild Ranger* fell into the occasional company of Chinese junks. The island chains in the area were known to be inhabited by pirates and unfriendly natives. Bethia feared that "they might pay us a visit," but the leg into Calcutta was uneventful. Exiting the China Sea, on May 11th, she wrote, "Never want to see the China Sea again." At one point, they were hailed by natives in a small boat who offered to pilot the ship through the straits. Elisha allowed a couple of them on board to assist in the passage up the dangerous waterway. Bethia wrote of their appearance. " I never shall forget how the natives looked that came in that boat. He (the senior native) certainly was very odd looking – tall and slender as a may-pole and hair all shaved very closely. They are very curious looking creatures and dress so queerly. A strip of cloth around their waists fastened by means of a handkerchief. A kind of frock around their waists and a long girdle or scarf put across their shoulders and fastened around the waist. And with turbans on their heads completed their attire... They chew some kind of seeds that makes their mouths look very red."[9]

From the Singapore Straits the ship entered the Straits of Malacca and the final run into the Bay of Bengal and on to Calcutta. Monsoon weather gave the *Wild Ranger* a stormy passage and Bethia compared it to Cape Horn and stated, "I don't know how I have lived through it all."

The *Wild Ranger* arrived in Calcutta on Tuesday, June 3, 1856. Bethia prepared the cabin area for the arrival of visitors, one of the first being another Brewster skipper, Captain William Low Foster.[10] He brought letters from home with him and persuaded Elisha to take a room in one of the city's hotels where other American captains stayed. Bethia made a rather unceremonial arrival on shore, having to be carried in a sedan chair from the ship's boat, across the mud flats to the roadway. While Elisha took care of ship's business, Bethia transferred her belongings to the hotel where she enjoyed the company of several sea captains' wives. She sewed with them and was feeling well enough to go on occasional shopping forays to the bazaars in the Indian city. She visited the zoo and saw the famous Bengal tigers housed there. On one occasion she recorded being taken to view the ghats where the dead bodies of Hindus were incinerated. "Saw three bodies burning, it was horrible, horrible."[11]

The *Wild Ranger* left Calcutta in the first week of August of 1856. Bethia was still experiencing a good deal of sickness. It may well have been in her already weakened condition, she fell victim to one of the many tropical illnesses that were associated with that port. Her journal mentions the presence of cholera and there are references to recent deaths of westerners from fever. She and Elisha were both troubled by bouts with dysentery and she had difficulty keeping food down. Soon after sailing, she came down with a fever and was delirious for a time. She did not make an entry in her journal until August 20th when she apparently felt well enough to sit up and make a brief notation. But it was another week before she put pen to paper again, still suffering from dysentery and considerable weight loss.

As August turned into September, Bethia became weaker and weaker. Her journal entries were irregular and brief. On September 16th she wrote, "I feel miserably at times. Do hope I shall be better before long. I do not take anything as I know not what to try."[12] This is the last entry that she made in her logbook. Ten days later Elisha noted her passing in his own hand, "My poor wifey is dead and gone." He recounted nursing her and at one point hailing a passing British vessel to bring a doctor to her side. But his young bride's survival was not to be. As he held her in his arms on September 26th, "she laid her head on my shoulder like a child going to sleep and died," were the words he used to describe the sad scene. "Oh yes, she died. I would not have believed it, no not when they took her away from me cold and stiff in death. Oh, if a mother could have been with her to close her eyes, or a sister to have wept with me – What a comfort it would have been – but no, I was all alone... why did she die – why has she been taken from me – Oh God have mercy."[13]

Elisha had a coffin built for Bethia so that her body could be returned to her family. All the rest of the day the crew came to the aft cabin to offer some solace to their captain. Each of them, wrote Elisha, in their own way, tried to "add some word of consolation for my poor breaking heart." For the rest of that day, the captain and crew of the *Wild Ranger* mourned for the loss of their delicate and popular shipmate.

Captain Elisha Freeman Sears returned home to Cape Cod and eventually remarried, becoming the father of three children. He served in the Union Navy for two years in the Civil War. Later he commanded transatlantic steamships and in 1870, transported a cargo of circus animals for P.T. Barnum in his *Erie*. For a time, he was superintendent of the Boston and Nantasket excursion boats. Captain Sears died on April 15, 1897 and is buried between his second wife Ellen Foster Sears and another stone marked for his first wife "Bethia," in the Lower Road cemetery in Brewster. As for the *Wild Ranger*, the clipper made many more successful runs in her career under a number of skippers. In the early years of the Civil War she was sold to British interests as were many American ships in the face of the threat of Confederate raiders like the *Alabama* and the *Florida*. In 1872, she collided with a steamship in the English Channel while on a voyage to Brazil and was lost.

• • •

Chapter XI

"We played ship and dolls and most all games we could think of."

CLARA FREEMAN OF BREWSTER

While there are a number of sea journals available that were compiled by adult women, it is unusual to find an account that was kept in real time by a child. Life at sea as it was observed through the eyes of a youngster was understandably quite different than it was viewed by adults. Most accounts that we have of children being aboard ship are observations made in a mother's journal. Or they may be reminiscences by older women who remembered their years as children at sea. In some journals we find accounts about the difficulty of keeping track of boisterous boys and girls on rolling decks and in foreign ports. Some child rearing issues remained the same, even for seagoing children.

Children were expected to continue their education while embarked aboard ship and parents handled the responsibility of monitoring lessons and teaching the values and skills that were part of nineteenth century life. Boys tended to be given a bit more freedom at sea and could often be found scrambling up the rigging in imitation of the crewmen. In a sense, they were being apprenticed as miniature sailors in preparation for the work that many of them would eventually end up doing. For girls, it was different. In an age where women were considered the more delicate of the sexes, girls tended to stay closer to their mothers while learning to master the domestic arts that the culture expected of them. It was a rare ship that gave daughters the liberty of the deck and in the case of those few that did allow girls more freedoms, they were still far more circumscribed than was the case with boys.

But what an experience it must have been for the children who went to sea with their parents. The exposure to extraordinarily different cultures that came with voyages around the world made seagoing children very different from children who remained at home. One historian has observed that many of the girls who went to sea never married. This, said the writer, may well have come from the fact that young men who had never seen much of life away from their own village were possibly intimidated by females who could converse about places and events that made a potential land-based suitor's life seem relatively dull. Unless there was the prospect of marrying a sea captain, to which these girls were ideally suited, the chances of marriage were probably lessened. At any rate, it was certainly true that many Cape Cod sons and daughters of sea captains could claim knowledge of a very wide range of places at a very young age. Theirs was an education by experience that had no equal on land.

Clara Freeman of Brewster, the ten-year old daughter of Captain William Freeman, was a faithful journal keeper during her voyage aboard her father's ship *Mogul* in 1873. On a ten-month trip from Wales to Rio de Janeiro, then to India, and finally back to England, Clara rarely missed an entry. Her account carries information that a child would be expected to record. Her pets, playmates, and games, as well as some impressions of foreign ports, are part of her experience aboard the *Mogul*. Her simple journal is a unique and rare eyewitness portrait of a child's sea experience.[1]

It was cold and raw as the ship *Mogul* left the port of Cardiff,

Captain William Freeman. Courtesy of Cape Cod Community College.

Wales in November of 1872. Captain William Freeman had a cargo of coal on board that was bound for the Brazilian port of Rio de Janeiro. He also had his wife Phebe and daughter Clara with him. This wasn't the first sea voyage for ten-year old Clara. The *Mogul* had been in Rangoon earlier in the year and Clara had many memories of the Far East. In truth she was more familiar with life aboard ship than she was with her large home in Brewster's town center.[2] She had her own small room on the *Mogul* and it was outfitted in much the same way as any young girl's room would have been on land. She also had several pets with her, including a cat named Tom, a goat, and a number of bantam hens that she had named.

The first weeks out from Cardiff saw the cold weather continuing and the seas rough. Clara, just as many of the adults aboard, was sick for a few days and she spent much of this time in her room. Water washing across the deck made it dangerous to go topside and she feared that her goat might be washed overboard. The *Mogul* eventually picked up a fair wind and Clara noted passing the Madeira Islands on November 25, 1872. The dark ocean night sky was an ideal place to see shooting stars and she spent hours at night in good weather with her father watching them. After a Thanksgiving dinner which featured "2 nice fowls," the ship entered the southern Trades where the weather warmed and the ship settled down to ride more easily.

Clara's daily routine at sea included some schoolwork and helping her mother sew and iron. It seemed that mending and fixing her father's clothing was a primary and never ending job. She mentioned the task often. "Anybody may think we work on shirts for Papa all the time," she wrote. "And if they did, they would not think wrong for I do not know how many shirts he has got."

It was always a happy occasion to see another ship on the broad ocean and it was with excitement on December 9th that Clara recorded their speaking the ship *Hartfell*, which was on its way to Calcutta. It was a chance to check longitude positions and to exchange letters and newspapers. The next day the *Mogul* crossed the equator. On December 12, 1872, when they spoke the ship *Centaur* bound for San Francisco, Clara noted, "She came so very near that we threw an apple on board." The first view of Brazil came on December 20th when the ship sighted Cape Frio and they were anchored in Rio de Janeiro the next day.

While the *Mogul* discharged its cargo of coal in the Brazilian port, Clara had the chance to go ashore with her parents. She recorded seeing many animals – monkeys, unusual birds, etc., and delighting in their strange colors and sounds. She played with other children who were visiting the port and her father erected a swing on the *Mogul* for their enjoyment. The Freemans spent Christmas and New Years in Rio entertaining and visiting with other American families that were anchored there. There were children aboard the ships *William* and *Ivanhoe* and she struck up a friendship with a Lillie Harding and the two girls met almost every day and "played ship and dolls and most all the games we could think of."[3] On January 2, 1873, Clara had her eleventh birthday. Her bantams were constantly laying eggs and she dutifully recorded each one as an important daily event.

The *Mogul* was ready for sea on February 10, 1873 and Captain Freeman set a course for India. The time in Rio had dulled her sea legs and again, Clara recorded being seasick for several of the first days back at sea. When she felt better, she occupied herself in sewing with her mother and making paper dolls. One of the crewmen died from yellow fever and was buried at sea on February 17th. Deaths at sea were usually times of great reflection by adult women who kept sea journals. Surprisingly, but perhaps explained by her young age, Clara made little mention of this event in her journal although the death and solemn commitment of the body to the sea certainly must have made quite an impression on her.

It grew colder as the ship tracked across the South Atlantic.

The Captain Freeman Home in Brewster, Massachusetts. Photo by Jim Coogan.

On February 28th they sighted the island of Tristan da Cunha and Clara noted that the change in the weather had brought out the stove. In a strong gale on March 10th, some of the ship's cargo broke loose and the crew had to work quickly to restow it to maintain the *Mogul*'s stability. As the ship pitched and rolled, Clara's mother badly damaged a finger when one of the interior doors in the aft cabin slammed shut on it. It was a long and rough period at sea in the Pacific before Ceylon was on the horizon on April 12th. The sewing project continued to produce seemingly endless mountains of clothing and Clara observed that "Moma is still at work on shirts and I believe when she gets this one done, it will be the 45th colored shirt she has made."

On April 25, 1873, the *Mogul* reached Bassein, India. To her delight, the *Ivanhoe* was also in port and Clara was able to play with some of the children that she had previously met in Rio de Janeiro. Ashore, she went on pony rides and acquired some new pets – several tropical birds and three turtle doves. They stayed in port for about two weeks unloading cargo and awaiting orders.

On May 8th, the *Mogul* got underway for a return to Falmouth, England. This was to be the longest leg of the voyage and Captain Freeman estimated that they would arrive sometime in mid-September. Shortly after leaving Bassein, near the Andaman Islands, Clara recorded seeing a total eclipse of the moon. It was about this time that she revealed that her father was having some trouble with a few of the members of the crew. "The cook, who has been troublesome all the passage," she noted. "Was so ugly that Papa was obliged to put him in irons for a short time." This is interesting because fourteen years earlier in 1859, as master of the ship *Undaunted*, Captain Freeman had been wounded while putting down a mutiny. Whether his daughter knew about that incident is not known, but she appears to have understood and accepted the need to discipline any rebellious member of the ship's crew.

As they re-crossed the equator in early June, Clara mentioned being plagued by hoards of mosquitoes and of seeing lots of sharks around the *Mogul*. She also had a bit of personal discomfort from a toothache that was taken care of by the ship's dentist – her father. "This morning Papa took my tooth out. But it did not hurt me much for it was loose." The long days of this leg of the voyage were passed with reading, writing school compositions, and more sewing. On June 29, 1873, they spoke the English ship *Star of Albion* bound for Calcutta from London. The next day they sighted the island of St. Helena. As they got closer to the British Isles, the crew began to straighten up the ship and during a painting detail, one crewman fell overboard. Clara saw it happen and recorded the successful

*Clara Freeman as a young woman.
Courtesy of the Brewster Historical Society.*

rescue. "About two o'clock this afternoon, a man got overboard. He was working over the side and he carelessly let the stage go down in the water and he was washed off. But as soon as father heard it he had them throw over the grating for him to get on but he could not get it and they got out the boat and got him."

The *Mogul* sighted Flores in the Azores on September 2, 1873 and made Falmouth, England on September 15th. When the mail was brought aboard, Clara learned of a family tragedy that had happened at home. "I regret to say we received bad news. My dear brother has lost his dear wife,"[4] she wrote without revealing much emotion. The *Mogul* spent just a few days in Falmouth before the ship received orders to sail to Dordrecht, Germany on the North Sea. Clara went shopping with her mother and was given the gift of two books written by Louisa May Alcott, "Little Women" and "Little Women Married." On the 18th of September the ship sailed for Dordrecht, a place that Clara had apparently visited before and indicated she didn't like. On the 21st of September the *Mogul* anchored at Bremerhaven and her father went ashore to communicate with the ship's owners by telegraph. As September ended, so did Clara's journal for the voyage.

The voyage on the *Mogul* had not been Clara Freeman's first time at sea, nor would it be her last. She continued to sail with her father and mother for quite a few more years. In the early 1880s, no longer a child, Clara became the first white woman to set foot on Pitcairn Island in the Pacific Ocean when her father's new command, the *Jabez Howes*, made a short stop there. Her subsequent friendship with an island girl, Rosalind Amelia Young, the granddaughter of Edward Young, one of the original *H.M.S. Bounty* mutineers, produced a longtime connection by correspondence between the two women who were products of very different worlds.

Clara's mother, Phebe, died in the summer of 1885. Captain Freeman lived to be ninety-one and was, for a time, the oldest resident of the town of Brewster. His days ended on April 1,

1911. Clara eventually worked for a time as a nurse, married, and moved to Bridgeport, Connecticut. When she died in September of 1926, she was buried next to her father, mother, and brother in the Lower Road Cemetery in Brewster. As for the fate of the ship *Mogul*, it caught fire in the Pacific on a run from Liverpool to San Francisco just a year after Clara's 1873 journal voyage. The ship was abandoned at sea on August 7, 1874. This time Clara and her mother were fortunately not aboard. Captain Freeman and his twenty-seven-member crew survived the sinking after being at the mercy of the sea for twelve days in the ship's three lifeboats and reaching the Marquesas, 2,100 miles away.

• • •

Chapter XII

*"I told him I lived in
Cape Cod in America"*

Sarah Priscilla Weekes of Harwich

Another young Cape Cod girl who went to sea early in her life was Sarah Priscilla Weekes of Harwich. Arriving in San Francisco after a long voyage from Liverpool, and asked where she was from, the six-year old proudly replied that she lived "in Cape Cod in America." She was aboard her father's ship, the *Mazeppa*, and already a veteran of the passage around Cape Horn and a seasoned sailor. The story of her sea adventure was set down in a small privately printed book, entitled *Two Years On Shipboard*, which she wrote as an adult in 1916. The fact that more than a half century had passed since the voyage does not dim the memories that Sarah held of her experiences as a child at sea. As a reminiscence, even though considerably removed from the actual experience, it contains much detail about family life at sea in the mid-nineteenth century. All quotes are from the forty-two page edition.

In 1862, the American Civil War had been raging for more than a year. Confederate raiding ships were taking their toll on Union shipping. The rebel raider *Alabama* was roaming the Atlantic, picking off unwary vessels and sinking them. Cape Codders were well aware of the dangers of making a sea voyage in these early years of the war. Two whaling schooners from Provincetown, the *Weather Gage* and the *Courser*, had already been sunk by the *Alabama* that summer. Thus, when a letter came to the Weekes' Harwichport home in the fall of 1862, it provoked considerable discussion and some concern. The correspondence was from Captain Darius Fessenden Weekes, a Harwich sea captain who was then in Liverpool, having finished a two-year voyage and awaiting orders. The captain's dilemma, as he wrote to his wife Rhoda, centered on his concern that if he were to return to the United States and visit with his family, he might be drafted into the military – a prospect that he did not fancy. Instead, he proposed that Rhoda and their young daughter Sarah take passage on a ship across the Atlantic and join him in Britain aboard his ship, the *Mazeppa*, for his next voyage.[1] Despite the obvious dangers of such a plan, Rhoda agreed to take passage on the steamer *China*, which was scheduled to sail in December of 1862, and meet her husband in Liverpool.

For a child who was not yet six years old, the scope of what her parents were planning was undoubtedly lost. Sarah remembered being bundled sleepily in the stagecoach and driven to the Yarmouth railroad depot where mother and child boarded the "cars" for the trip to New York City. Once aboard the steamer *China*, they slipped down the harbor past the battery on December 19, 1862. It was a ten-day passage to Liverpool, marked by snow squalls and rain. Sarah's mother was sick most of the voyage, a passage that the little girl recalled as "dreary and anxious." But Sarah was in the care of a maid and enjoyed the attention of the passengers who were charmed and entertained by this smallest of sailors.

Captain Weekes met Rhoda and Sarah in Liverpool, just after Christmas. It had been two years since he had seen them and the reunion was a joyous one. Sarah was brought aboard the *Mazeppa* and settled into what would be her seagoing home for the next two years. She remembered being delighted with the accommodations,

Captain Darius F. Weekes. Courtesy of Sturgis Library.

Rhoda Weekes. Courtesy of Sturgis Library.

noting that she had her own stateroom, which was off the main salon of the after cabin. An adjacent compartment served as a storeroom, and it was filled with fresh fruit, nuts, and canned goods. In particular, the presence of a cage of canaries that was suspended from the overhead fascinated her. One of them had been trained to do tricks and Sarah was allowed to take the bird out for play time.

A few of the crewmembers were Cape Codders. Lysander Taylor from South Harwich was the ship's steward and was billeted in the forward cabin where the family and the mates took their meals. He made special care to look after Sarah's needs and became a good friend.

The *Mazeppa* finished loading a cargo of coal and set sail for San Francisco on January 16, 1863. The ship ran into heavy gales and broke her rudder, necessitating putting into Bristol, England for repairs. They put to sea again on February 17th in better weather conditions and made good time to the south coast of Spain where the *Mazeppa* briefly stopped off Gibraltar to drop letters in the large watertight floating cask that was chained to a rock there. Sarah posted a letter to her uncle James Small of Harwichport. It was received back on Cape Cod several weeks later.

Once out in the broad Atlantic, Sarah busied herself in learning the routine of a ship. She watched the men at work and "walked decks," being careful to stay behind the chalk line that was aft of the galley – a line that separated where the crew lived from the family spaces. She played with the ship's dog and cat and practiced coiling lines as the sailors did. When stormy weather kept her below, she worked on her sewing and her studies. Even at five years old, she had lessons in arithmetic and reading. She used a slate to mark her letters and sang songs with her mother. The young sailor learned to play cribbage with her father and took the opportunity to go "coasting" on the cabin floor when the ship's motion created a sufficient roll to do so. "It was great fun for me," she recalled. "But mother watched the

The Mazeppa. *Courtesy of Sturgis Library.*

game disapprovingly, as it was somewhat detrimental to some parts of my clothing." Sarah began a collection of delicate seaweeds that were pressed as patterns into a small scrapbook.

   Occasionally, the *Mazeppa* "spoke" passing vessels at sea. Sarah watched the crew hoisting signal flags on a halyard and wondered if she might eventually master the combinations of flags and be able one day to send a message of her own. On May 15th, the ship passed around Cape Horn, and Sarah caught a brief glimpse of land in the mist. Heavy seas pummeled the vessel and she recalled that the ship was almost buried in the mighty waves. She spent much of the passage around the Horn "huddled up in the wide berth, talking and singing, now and then staggering out to an uncomfortable meal." She also noted that the reefs were not out of the sails for over a month, indicating the strength of the winds. At one point, the ship's cabin boy, an Italian named "Bumbo," was almost washed overboard and was only saved by Sarah's father, who grabbed the boy just before he went over the rail. "Bumbo" later fell down a hatchway and broke his arm. Captain Weekes put him in the after cabin where Sarah saw quite a bit of him during his confinement. Even though she tried to make friends with him, the experience wasn't a good one. "...he stole a silver rupee, a piece of English money, and left in its place, a lead rupee, which I now have, a treasured relic, but I lost all further interest in him or his musical language."

The *Mazeppa* arrived in San Francisco on August 15, 1863 after a passage of more than six months from Liverpool. As the ship unloaded its cargo of coal, Sarah went ashore to reacquaint her feet with solid ground. She made day trips with her mother into the city and visited the Zoological Gardens where she was especially fascinated by the snakes. The time in port was fairly short and when the ship sailed for Peru, Sarah found it difficult to get back to a ship's routine.

Sailing in ballast with a few passengers, the *Mazeppa* left San Francisco on September 16th and arrived again in Callao, Peru on November 1, 1863. One of the passengers, a Senor Mendiola, who Sarah described as "a true Spanish gentleman," taught her a little Spanish. The language came in handy when she and her mother were billeted in the American Hotel in Callao. The owner of the hotel had four children and Sarah's pidgin Spanish let her make friends with them quickly. Captain Weekes had reason to put Rhoda and Sarah up in more permanent quarters. His wife was in her eighth month of pregnancy and the captain did not wish to chance a birth in less than ideal conditions at sea. Leaving his wife and daughter in Callao, Captain Weekes sailed on November 12th for the Chincha Islands, about one hundred miles to the south of the city, to load guano. In the company of friends and other American families, Sarah went on a number of excursions out of Callao. On one occasion, she visited the city of Lima, Peru's capital.

Sarah at age six in San Fransisco. Courtesy of Sturgis Library.

Another time she ventured far inland to a Spanish city that had been destroyed in an earthquake a century earlier. While Sarah was in Callao there were several small quakes, severe enough for the hotel to shake and sway.

In early December, Rhoda gave birth to a little girl. Sarah noted that "the event" produced a four-pound baby that was given the name "Rosita" as an honor to the landlord's wife who assisted in caring for Sarah and her mother.[2] Despite the fact that the newborn was underweight and soon developed a bad case of whooping cough, Rhoda, the baby, and Sarah went aboard an American ship that was headed for the Chinchas on December 12th. Once there, they rejoined Captain Weekes aboard the *Mazeppa* and waited at anchorage with ten other ships to take on the cargo of bird manure.

There was no opportunity to go ashore in the three-island Chincha group. There was no real town to speak of and no pier to tie up to. Loading the guano took a good bit of time. The odorous fertilizer was brought out to the waiting ships in barges and craned aboard and into the hold. But Sarah had the chance to visit with other families aboard some of the ships and there were children to play with. She noted that a ship arrived from Calcutta with a giant sea turtle in tow. The creature was killed and made into dinner for the flotilla. "The meat of a turtle of this kind," she recalled, "is of varied qualities and may be served as fish, flesh, or fowl. The green fat is used for the famous turtle soup, which is a great delicacy. It was a great occasion and a rare treat." The smelly cargo, which burned the eyes with ammonia fumes, however, didn't do much for Sarah's appraisal of the Chincha anchorage, particularly when the yellow dust blew in through the cabin windows. "We were told that if the dust from the guano settled on the head, it would cause the hair to fall out, so we tied up our heads in handkerchiefs." This might actually have been true. One writer who visited the Chinchas in this period noted that "Only fleas and lizards are indifferent to its ammonical properties."[3]

At last, the *Mazeppa* sailed again for Callao on February 14, 1864, the fresh breezes much appreciated by everyone after such a long confinement at the Chinchas. Captain Weekes picked up his orders to take the guano to Antwerp, Belgium and on February 20th they set a course for the Horn and Europe. The passage round Cape Horn was uneventful, but once into the Atlantic, the *Mazeppa* ran into the doldrums near the equator. From mid-March through mid-April, the ship lay becalmed, as Sarah put it, like "a painted ship on a painted ocean." Food supplies began to run out and the crew was put on short rations. After several weeks, the crew massed outside the captain's cabin and demanded more and better food. The mood of the rebellious men was angry. Captain Weekes pointed out that his own family wasn't faring any better, noting that they were eating "salt horse" and hard tack, just like the rest of them and not much of that. He invited several of the ringleaders into his cabin to show them that there was no extra food in the family quarters and for a time, this seemed to quiet the crew.

But less than a week later, the crew again demonstrated, and this time there was clearly a mutinous intent as they came aft with knives and clubs. Supported by his officers, Captain Weekes confronted the mutineers and a hand to hand fight ensued. The captain knocked down a few of the men with his brass knuckles and the mates weighed in with their fists. At one point, one of the mates raised a pistol to shoot a crewman but Rhoda's entreaties against this action stayed his hand. The chastened crew, recognizing that it was probably the captain's wife that had saved at least a few of them from death, were subdued and the ringleaders placed in irons. For the rest of the trip across the Atlantic, half the crew worked above decks under guard in a "port and starboard" arrangement, while the other half was locked below in the forecastle.

Only a single milk goat was left along with "Old Biddie" the hen as a source of milk and eggs. To keep the hen laying, Rhoda and Sarah made a mash out of ground buttons, which they fed to the half starved chicken. The goat survived on pieces of grass cloth from Sarah's petticoats. To further compound their situation, the *Mazeppa* was visited in mid-ocean by a "white squall," probably a severe frontal weather passage, and some oof the sails were shredded and spars broken. Several days were spent sewing bits of cloth into the frayed sails so that the ship could maintain course. With a number of sailors exhibiting signs of scurvy, the *Mazeppa* finally made the Isle of Wight off the coast of Wales in mid-July. While the mates kept the crew in order, Captain Weekes went ashore there and successfully bartered for food for his starving men. "We were reduced almost to skeletons," Sarah recalled. "But the good food revived us, and little Rosita, who was only a little bunch of bones, revived somewhat with good milk to drink once more."

It was July 20, 1864 when the *Mazeppa* entered the River Sheldt and the port of Antwerp where the talk of the city was of the recent sea battle off the French coast between the *U.S.S. Kearsarge* and the Confederate raider, *Alabama*. Barely able to carry themselves to the hotel in their emaciated state, the Weekes family settled in to recover from the lengthy and difficult Atlantic passage. Captain Weekes spent the majority of the time supervising the ship's unloading and after several weeks of restoring strength, he took Rhoda and Sarah to see some of the sights of the Belgian city. During the two-month stay there, the family shopped and toured the many attractions.

In September, Captain Weekes was informed that the *Mazeppa* was to be sold to new owners and that he should put himself and his family on a ship back to Boston for another command. They arrived in Liverpool and sailed for home aboard the steamer Delaware on October 1, 1864, arriving in Boston after a ten-day passage.[4] Captain Weekes, Rhoda, Sarah, and little Rosita took the train to Hyannis and finished their journey to Harwichport via stagecoach. There they were met by five-year old Letella, the daughter that had been left with relatives in Falmouth. The family moved in with Sarah's grandparents, Mr. and Mrs. Philip Small, until their new home in South Harwich was completed in the spring of 1865.

In the years following the Civil War, Captain Darius Weekes stayed close to his new home in Harwich. For nine years he was in the fish packing business on the coast at "Deep Hole" in South Harwich. He also grew cranberries and in 1887, he was elected Deputy Sheriff of Barnstable County. He died at his Harwich home on April 22, 1911. Rhoda died on May 14, 1923 at age eighty-seven. Sarah eventually married Judah E. Foster of Brewster in 1878 and not long after moved with her husband to Newport, Vermont, where she spent the rest of her life. Little Rosita never regained her strength from the arduous sea journey and died in the spring of 1865. All of the family except for Sarah are buried in the family plot in South Harwich.

• • •

Chapter XIII

"The shoals and quicksands of life require a vigilant watch"

SALLY MAYO DYER LAVENDER OF PROVINCETOWN

Thus was the view of the world according to the wife of Provincetown Captain Joseph Richardson Lavender as she assessed her life aboard the 158-ton brig *Panama* during a voyage to Europe to pick up a cargo of fruit. Sally Mayo Dyer Lavender was a highly moralistic lady who gives every indication that she did not enjoy her seagoing days even though she made a number of transatlantic voyages in the 1850s.[1] Born in 1826 to Henry Dyer and his wife of Provincetown, Sally was one of ten children. Her transcribed journal, entitled, "A Journal of a Voyage from Boston to Marseilles," which is held at the Pilgrim Monument Museum in Provincetown, is a daily account of a four-month voyage that she made with her husband and seven-year old son William in the spring and summer of 1854. Her style is reflective and expresses a number of spiritual metaphors in describing her routine at sea.

The Mediterranean fruit trade had been a part of the commercial maritime activities of New England merchantmen from the early part of the nineteenth century. Competition between the ports of Boston and New York was strong as traders frequented outlets in southern France, Italy, Greece, and Turkey for fruit products. The trade involved two kinds of cargo, the first being what was termed "dry," consisting primarily of raisins and figs. The second, or "wet" variety involved trade in oranges and lemons. Merchant ships left American ports carrying logwood, used to add color to Mediterranean wines, and mahogany, tobacco, sugar, beeswax, and "domestics," which would have included materials from New England cotton mills. And there was always demand for New England rum.

Captain John Richardson Lavender and his brother, Captain Joseph Atkins Lavender, were two Provincetown shipmasters who were involved in the fruit trade in the 1850s and 60s. Both men had been born in Nova Scotia, the tenth and eleventh children of Robert and Ann Allin Lavender. In the 1840s they moved to Provincetown and married local women. Joseph Lavender married Clarissa Atwood in December of 1847 and she went with him on a number of trips to the Mediterranean. John Lavender married Sally Mayo Dyer a year earlier and there is good evidence that she accompanied her husband on a number of voyages. At one point in her journal she refers to having entered the Gulf Stream fourteen times, indicating at least seven Atlantic trips. She had sailed the previous year to Palermo, Italy aboard the *Panama* and was familiar with Mediterranean ports.

The voyage that has given us the only known journal kept by Sally Lavender commenced in March of 1854 when the *Panama* was ready to depart Provincetown for the open ocean. The ship had been fitted out and loaded in Boston and arrived at the Cape tip to pick up Sally and her young son. It was Sunday, March 12th, when the ship hauled anchor. Sally busied herself in the aft cabin reflecting on the upcoming Atlantic crossing and listening to the church bells ringing in town. It was a sound that brought home to her all too clearly the fact that she would be observing an unconventional string of Sabbaths for the next few months. Sally

Provincetown as Sally Lavender would have seen it. The town hall was located on High Pole Hill, the present site of the Pilgrim Monument. The town was a busy whaling ans shipping port in the mid 1800s. Courtesy of Cape Cod Community College.

sat at the cabin table and made her first entry on a clean page. "We were soon underway and leaving our native town far behind: for the vessel seemed to think that by her going it was not worth while to be long in leaving Provincetown and as if there were more pleasing scenes ahead."

The season of the fruit traders made a late-winter departure necessary so as to arrive at the peak of the season in Europe. March in the Atlantic Ocean still features its share of winter's fury and the *Panama* spent half of the five-week crossing in fierce gales and stormy weather. Just three days out Sally was trying to adjust to the rolling deck and took a few moments to write some lines. "This day finds us still hurrying on with a westerly wind which makes it very pleasant if my stomach does not rise up against it and make me throw up all the good things I eat. But never mind, it won't be long that I shall mind her rolling."

Rough weather caused problems in the aft cabin. "I was pleased in watching our steward when he came below to clear away the breakfast table which by the way needed him sadly for the dishes did not possess attraction of gravitation sufficient to adhere to the places destined for them..." For the rest of the week, Sally ate her food while sitting on the floor of the cabin so as not to be tossed around the space. Sleeping was no easier as the ship pounded eastward. "I clung to the sides [of the berth] to prevent being thrown out and for a moment I am lost. I hardly know whether I am in the berth or on the floor... The wind is now howling fiercely through our rigging and the angry waves are dashing against her sides as if they were punishing her for some misconduct" To compound Sally's discomfort, it was cold enough that the ship encountered icebergs about 800 miles out.

On March 28th, the *Panama* reached the Azores. The weather had moderated and Sally recorded days of sewing her husband's clothes and reading from her well stocked library. The ship had overtaken several east bound vessels and she confessed some guilt at passing them, acknowledging that their time at sea would be longer than hers. In one of her spiritual metaphors, she compared her sea voyage to her own life's voyage. "...I beheld in the distance several sail on the way to their destined ports, or perhaps to the places that are to become their watery graves; for while we are in life we are in death and as we hasten on to various ports know not how fast we are approaching our final end."

Off Cape Vincent, Portugal, on April 8th, she made her first and only mention of her son, William. "Had quite a fine time with my little boy playing 'hide and seek' for he must have someone to play with once in awhile." That she was lonely is quite clearly revealed in a number of entries in her journal. She nevertheless viewed her isolation with a stoic acceptance, noting, "We are excluded from society but we form a society among ourselves. We are a little world of our own; have our own government; enact our own laws and see that they are obeyed and we make quite a pleasant community."

The sea approaches to the Straits of Gibraltar were difficult to navigate and Captain Lavender had to tack ship for several days before getting a fair wind that would allow the *Panama* to enter the Mediterranean. Sally noted that there were over eighty vessels maneuvering off the Moroccan coast – all looking for acceptable winds that could carry them through the straits.

The *Panama* spoke the American bark *Prompt* out of Boston on April 13th and another American ship, the *Rosebud*, the next day. Flies didn't help the atmosphere aboard the ship and Sally compared their biting to be as bad as Cape Cod mosquitoes. It wasn't until April 23, 1854, after six weeks at sea, that she could look out at Marseilles, France.

There were over two-hundred vessels anchored in the southern French port. "Their masts look like trees in a forest with the rigging for foliage," she noted. Even though the early spring dampness brought a chill to the cabin, no fires were allowed aboard any of the closely positioned ships because of the fear that a fire might sweep through the anchorage. Sally had been in Marseilles before and knew where she wanted to shop – and which merchants offered the best prices. She was adept at bargaining with them and complimented herself on being a shrewd shopper. Local women came on board the *Panama* and took off laundry, giving her a welcome respite from that chore. She enjoyed Marseilles for about two weeks before the ship departed for Catania, Sicily.

While enroute to Sicily, Sally observed the active volcano Stromboli as it belched smoke and fire and she commented on the size and beauty of Mount Etna as they passed its imposing height. In Catania, she was struck by the apparent poverty of the place and the number of beggars that lined the quay. "One can hardly go a dozen steps without having a hand thrust in the way and a motion made with the other to the mouth..." Showing a Protestant bias, she blamed the situation on the control of society by the Church, accusing the priests of keeping the people poor. The Italian church hierarchy lived, in Sally's view, "a life of idleness and sin."

Over the week and a half in Catania that Sally spent there, the *Panama* was loaded with six hundred boxes of lemons, brimstone, sumac, canary seeds, and bales of rags. For some reason, oranges were in short supply and Captain Lavender was unable to obtain any to bring home to America. Sally, for her part, mentioned no social engagements or outings with her husband or her son while in the Italian city. She seems to have been content, for the most part, to stay aboard reading. Shortly after the ship departed on May 27th, some of the cargo apparently began to spoil, giving off noxious smells that made everyone on board sick with "the bowel complaint." Unfavorable winds continued to plague the progress of the voyage and they bucked hard westerlies for the first several weeks.

The *Panama* entered the Atlantic on June 21st and conditions improved. Summer weather made it possible for Sally to spend extended time up on the deckhouse reading and sewing. On June 24th, they spoke the Europe bound American bark *Turk*, twenty-seven days out from Boston. Near the Azores, the crew captured and killed a killer whale, which was taken aboard and butchered for dinner. Sally, however, decided that whale meat was not for her. "It furnished a rich repast for all on board excepting myself; for I was so foolish, I dare not taste of it although it sent forth a most delicious odor and certainly looked very nice." Later, in mid-ocean, she did eat part of a dolphin.

The final leg of the voyage saw the *Panama* becalmed in 90-degree temperatures. Rain was scarce and the threat of water rationing was considered by the captain. Traveling in fog much of the time, the clouds lifted briefly on July 21st and around six o'clock in the late afternoon Sally got a glimpse of Highland Light. Fog and light breezes, however, forced the *Panama* to hove to for the night. "If there had been a good breeze, we should have been in Boston as snug as a bug in a rug," she lamented in one of her last entries. The next day, after a trip of four months and nine days, the voyage was completed in Boston Harbor.

After the American Civil War, Captain John Lavender went into the "commission" fruit business at Meragoane, Haiti, where he died of heart disease on June 9, 1878, at age fifty-five. Records show that he moved his family from the Cape tip to Melrose, Massachusetts after the war. While he was buried in Haiti, there is no record that his wife accompanied him to that Caribbean island. His job may have been seasonal. Sally Lavender died in Melrose on April 28, 1915, at the age of eighty-eight. She was brought back to Provincetown by her surviving sons, William and John, for burial. The marriage had produced five children, three sons and two daughters. As for the not often mentioned son William, he eventually spent some time at sea as captain in his own right and finished his days as the city treasurer in Melrose.

• • •

Acknowledgments

Writing a book like this is really a group effort. Without the assistance and resources that were made available to me by many people, I think it would be safe to say that there would have been no book at all. Having access to a number of excellent libraries and private collections was perhaps most important. The William Brewster Nickerson Cape Cod history collection, located in the library at Cape Cod Community College in West Barnstable, was probably my starting point over twenty-five years ago. Over that time librarian/archivists, Herbert McKenney, Charlotte Price, and Mary Sicchio always made sure that I had materials that related to my focus area. It seemed that whatever I asked for, they had something for me. The Sturgis Library in Barnstable, particularly its Henry Crocker Kittredge maritime collection, was also important. The microfilm collection of the *Barnstable Patriot* and *Yarmouth Register* newspapers that are housed at Sturgis provided excellent backup supplements to journals and logbooks. It was in the Sturgis Library that I discovered, quite by accident, the sea account of Sarah Weekes. The Brooks Library in Harwich was also a source for microfilm of the *Harwich Independent* newspaper. Historical societies in Brewster, Dennis, Sandwich, Yarmouth, Harwich, and Falmouth opened their archives to me.

In 1996, I was selected by the Massachusetts Council for the Humanities as a Scholar in Residence at the Provincetown Heritage Museum. That summer, under that sponsorship, I was able to access the collections from both the Heritage Museum and the Pilgrim Monument Museum. Dale Fanning, then director of the Provincetown Heritage Museum, eased my way around the town library collection, which included the microfilm collection of the *Provincetown Advocate*, and the holdings of the two museums at the Cape tip. I used the Boston Public Library as an additional source of microfilm for various nineteenth century newspapers. The Phillips Library, part of the Peabody Essex Museum in Salem, Massachusetts, provided good information about Bethia Sears and her voyage aboard her husband's clipper, the *Wild Ranger*. Britta Karlberg and Irene Axelrod assisted me in finding and using the materials there.

A number of people made family journals, letters, and diaries available to me. Some of these materials had never been reviewed or published in any other form. Georgia Knowles Ferguson of Barnstable arranged for me to interview her ninety-seven year old mother Carrie Knowles, who in 1982, was still able to remember information about the Provincetown of her youth and some stories about Viola Cook. Lurana Cook of Truro gave me details about Viola's last sad days. David and Nancy Sears of East Dennis provided background on Persis Addy and a copy of her letter from Samoa. In the 1980's, I interviewed Mildred Crowell, the ninety-four year old daughter of little "Lulu" Sears, also of East Dennis, who told me about her mother's pony rides aboard the clipper ship *Wild Hunter* and of the seagoing experiences of her grandmother Minerva Sears.

Jim Carr of Dennis provided a picture of Persis Addy and

also let me use a photograph that he took in Hong Kong of the grave of Captain Benjamin Perkins Howes. Mrs. Ralph Manning of Winchester, Massachusetts, a great-great-granddaughter of Clara Cook Ryder, allowed me to have access to photographs of the family and a transcribed copy of Clara's logbook. Mrs. Manning was generous enough to meet me at the family house in Provincetown where I saw where Clara and her husband Stephen actually lived. Robert Coleman of Orleans invited me to his home to look at scrapbooks and letters related to Captain Bennett Coleman and Robert's grandmother, Edith Nickerson Coleman. His sister, Nancy Coleman Wyman provided me with a picture of Edith Nickerson Coleman.

Jane Baxter of Centerville gave me a transcribed copy of the unpublished seagoing diary of her great grandmother, Rebecca Wood Howes of South Yarmouth, which had been edited by her late Aunt Anne Hall Baxter. She was a wonderful source of photographs of both Rebecca and husband Barnabas and she passed around my draft to other members of the family for verification. Andrew and Sally Tournas invited me into the house in South Yarmouth where Rebecca was born and where she and Barnabas lived and they let me look at some of the many letters preserved by Sally's family that were written by Rebecca to her husband and to her mother.

Gerry Watters, of El Cajon, California, the great granddaughter of Lucy Lord Howes, added information about the 1866 pirate attack on the *Lubra* from her new book, *Privateers, Pirates, and Beyond: Memoirs of Lucy Lord Howes Hooper*, and also verified my summary of that tragic story. I also used the Lucy Lord Howes materials which are stored at the Massachusetts Historical Society archives on Boyleston Street in Boston. Bonnie Snow of Orleans kept me straight on the many branches of the Knowles family. Ellen St. Sure of Brewster, a relative of the Sears family, proofread and verified information about Bethia Sears. Other proofreaders were Jim Carr, Judy Friend, Beth Friend, and Martha Zimmerman.

Yarmouthport artist Caroline Ellis provided original paintings that were incorporated on the back cover as well as within the text. Syracuse University Press allowed me to use material from *The Capn's Wife* by Albert Joseph George. Philip Weimerskirch of the Providence Public Library sent me the microfilm of Mary Chipman Lawrence's *Addison* journal, saving me considerable time and effort in putting together her story.

As always, Jack Sheedy, my editor and co-publisher, and Jackie Rockwell, the graphic designer, were the rocks that I clung to in the final stages of finishing the work. Special thanks to Adriana Sheedy who spent long hours smoothing the text and assisting in the final page format. To all of them, institutions and individuals, I owe a debt of gratitude in the writing of this book.

Notes

Introduction

1 From the archives of the Historical Society of Old Yarmouth. Other excerpts of letters between Anna and her husband are summed up in an article by Margaret Milliken, "Letters to Captain Bangs Hallet on his voyage to Calcutta, 1859-60," printed in *The Register*, December 22, 1977, Section II, p. 1.

2 Harwich Historical Society archives.

Chapter 1. Experiences of Life at Sea

1 Taken from an original copy of Clara Cook Ryder's journal, located at the Pilgrim Monument and Provincetown Museum. The journal was donated to the museum by Mrs. Ralph Manning of Winchester, MA. Mrs. Manning is the great-great-granddaughter of Clara Cook Ryder.

2 This story came from an undated edition of the *New Bedford Standard Times* from around 1935. The clipping is held by the Provincetown Heritage Museum. Information about the sailing career of the *Ellen A. Swift* came from *Returns of Whaling Vessels Sailing From American Ports: 1876-1928*, compiled by Reginald B. Hegarty, the Old Dartmouth Historical Society and Whaling Museum, New Bedford, MA, 1959.

3 *Ibid.*

4 From a letter dated January 28, 1867 sent by Persis Addy to her parents. Courtesy of David and Nancy Sears.

5   *The Yarmouth Register*, article by Theodore W. Swift August 17, 1935.

6   *Descendants of Richard Knowles 1637-1973*, Virginia Knowles Hufbauer, Ventures International publishers, San Diego, CA, 1974, p. 483, 484.

7   *Cape Cod Magazine*, May 15, 1927, p. 8.

8   *A Sea Trip in Clipper Ship Days*, by Mary Matthews Bray, Richard G. Badger ed., The Gorham Press, Boston, MA., 1920, p. 63.

9   *Seafaring Women*, by Linda Grant De Pauw, Houghton Mifflin Co., Boston, MA., 1982, p. 150.

10 *Yarmouth Register*, article by Theodore W. Swift, February 16, 1935.

11 "Women Who Went to Sea," by Ora A. Hinkley, published in *Sand in Their Shoes: A Cape Cod Reader*, by Edith and Frank Shay, Houghton Mifflin Co., Boston, MA., 1951, p. 235.

12 *Cape Cod Remembrances*, by Marion Crowell Ryder, William S. Sullwold, blishing, Taunton, MA, 1972, p. 123.

13 Ryder, *Remembrances*, p. 110.

14 *History of Bourne: From 1622-1937*, by Betsy D. Keene, Charles W. Swift, publisher,Yarmouthport, MA, 1937, p. 85.

15 *Cape Cod Chronicle*, an article by Tim Wood, "Letter Details Tragic Loss of a Child At Sea in 1856," July 20, 1995. Based on letters in the possession of Julia Harding's great grandaughter, Nancy Olson of Chatham.

16 Ellis papers, Harwich Historical Society, from Georgia Knowles Ferguson.

17 *Bertha Goes Whaling*, by Bertha Hamblin Boyce, Kendall Printing Co., Falmouth, MA, 1963, p. 13.

18 Ryder, *Remembrances*, p. 122.

19 *Harwich Men of the Sea*, Harwich Historical Commission, Harwich, MA, 1977, p. 39.

20 *Dennis, Cape Cod: From First Comers to Newcomers 1639-1993*, by Nancy Thacher Reid, Published by the Dennis Historical Society, Dennis, MA, 1996, p. 382.

21 Journal of Sally Mayo Lavender, Pilgrim Memorial Museum, Provincetown, MA.

22 Personal letters of Mary Knowles, Brewster archives, Brewster Historical Society.

23 Ryder Journal, Provincetown.

24 "Women Who Went To Sea," by Ora A. Hinckley, in *Sand In Their Shoes: A Cape Cod Reader*, edited by Edith and Frank Shay, Houghton Mifflin Co., Boston, MA, 1951, p. 237.

25 *Barnstable: Three Centuries of a Cape Cod Town*, by Donald Trayser, F.B. & F.P. Goss, Hyannis, MA, 1939, p. 311.

26 Letters of Emily Crosby Lincoln, as published in *The Prolific Pencil*, by Persy Felitz Rex, edited by Fredrika A. Burrows, William S. Sullwold Publishing, Inc., Taunton, MA, 1980, p. 31.

27 Lavender Journal, Provincetown.
28 Lavender Journal, Provincetown.
29 *Barnstable and Yarmouth Sea Captains and Shipowners*, by Francis William Sprague, privately printed, Brookline, MA., 1913.
30 Lavender Journal, Provincetown.
31 Burgess Journal, April 13, 1856, Sandwich Historical Society.
32 Diary of Rebecca Wood Howes, transcribed by Anne Hall Baxter from the original, December 1972.
33 *The Cap'n's Wife*, by Albert Joseph George, Syracuse University Press, 1946. p62.
34 *Harwich Men of the Sea*, published by the Harwich Historical Commission, Harwich, MA, 1977, p. 45.
35 Ryder, *Remembrances* p. 108.
36 Burgess Journal, Sandwich Historical Society.
37 *Boston Globe*, December 24, 1905.
38 From the personal papers of Edith Nickerson Coleman, used through the courtesy of her grandson, Robert Coleman of Orleans, MA.

Chapter 2. Mary Chipman Lawrence of Falmouth

1 Mary Chipman Lawrence Journal, Nicholson Collection, Providence Public Library, (microfilm) Volumes I & II. p. 18. Vol I.
2 Journal, p. 19. Vol I.
3 Journal, p. 4. Vol I.
4 Journal, p. 13,14. Vol. I.
5 Journal, p. 20. Vol I.
6 Even though Mary received occasional correspondence from the four other women who were with their husbands in the Arctic that summer, she never was able to actually visit with any of them during the five-month cruise.
7 Journal, p. 30. Vol I.
8 Journal, p. 63. Vol. I
9 Journal, p. 65. Vol. I. Mary's willingness to express her views openly about how slow the Christianizing of the islanders was going came back to haunt her when she later read some of her opinions in a missionary journal which implied that she didn't think that the evangelizing efforts were bearing much fruit. She was embarrassed that her thoughts had surfaced in print form.
10 Journal. p. 158. Vol I.
11 Journal. p. 158.. Vol I.
12 Journal. p. 22. Vol. II.
13 Journal. p. 28. Vol. II.
14 Journal. p. 38. Vol. II.

15 Journal. p. 47. Vol. II.
16 Journal. p. 48. Vol. II.
17 Journal. p. 55. Vol. II.

Chapter 3. Ulah Harding Reed of Chatham
1 *The Cape Codder* newspaper, November 6, 1947, Orleans, MA, page 5.
2 *Ibid.*, p. 5.
3 *Ibid.*, p. 5.
4 *The Cape Codder* newspaper, November 27, 1947, Orleans, MA, page 6.
5 *Ibid.*, p. 5.

Chapter 4. Persis Crowell Addy of Dennis
1 Old Home Week brochure, July 26-August 2, 1942, Dennis Historical Society.
2 In a letter posted on August 31, 1866, she mentions having entertained a Captain and Mrs. Hallet from Barnstable, while in Shanghai.
3 Transcribed letter dated January 28, 1867, from Persis to her mother and father. The letter is in the possession of David and Nancy Sears of East Dennis, MA.
4 *Ibid.*
5 *Ibid.* The reference to "Henry" is to Captain John Henry Addy, her husband.
6 *Dennis, Cape Cod: From Firstcomers to Newcomers 1639-1993*, by Nancy Thacher Reid, Published by the Dennis Historical Society, Dennis, MA, 1996, p. 385.

Chapter 5. Lucy Lord Howes of Dennis
1 Henry Hall's account was published in the *Yarmouth Register* on Friday, March 1, 1867, on page 2.

Chapter 6. Rebecca Wood Howes of South Yarmouth
1 Rebecca Howes was a prolific letter writer. Many of her letters to her mother and to her husband over a period of several years are part of the archives collection of the Historical Society of Old Yarmouth in Yarmouth Port, MA.
2 *American Clipper Ships 1833-1858*, by Octavius T. Howe and Frederick C. Matthews, Dover Publications, Inc., New York, N.Y., Volume II, pages 643-646.

Chapter 7. Clara Cook Ryder of Provincetown
1 The *N.D. Chase* was a 241-ton vessel that had been built in Pembroke, Maine in 1847. She had served as a whaling ship as early as 1851 and was on her fifth expedition under Captain Ryder in 1857. The *N.D. Chase* was homeported in Beverly, MA, but often sailed from Provincetown. See *Whaling and Old Salem*, by Francis Diane Robotti, Fountainhead Publishers, New York, N.Y., 1962.

2   The original copy of Clara Cook Ryder's journal is located in the Pilgrim Monument Museum in Provincetown. It was donated to the museum by Mrs. Ralph Manning of Winchester, Massachusetts who was the great-great-granddaughter of Clara Cook Ryder. The logbook is not complete, covering only the first year of the two-year voyage. All quotes, unless otherwise noted, come from this transcribed copy of the journal.

3   Apparently, Captain Doyle was having some difficulty with his crew. Clara noted that he came aboard the *N.D. Chase* on July 22 "to get some firearms as his crew undertook to take the schooner the day before." Several subsequent entries have Captain Doyle staying the night aboard the *N.D. Chase*, rather than returning to his own ship.

4   Cintra Bay was named by the Portugese explorer Pedro de Cintra when he visited it in 1462. It is now part of the west African country of Sierra Leone.

5   The circumstance of Frank Ryder's death are covered in a letter dated September 6, 1876, from Captain Benjamin Sparks to Captain Stephen A. Ryder. The letter is in the possession of Mrs. Ralph Manning.

Chapter 8. Viola Fish Cook of Provincetown

1   *Boston Sunday Globe*, December 24, 1905.

2   In 1895, Viola was joined by Flora Whitesides on the *Belvedere*, Caroline Sherman on the *Beluga*, Sophia Porter on the *Wanderer*, Marion Smith on the *Narwhal*, and Fanny Weeks on the *Thrasher*. Mrs. Weeks' husband would die in a fall into the hold of his ship that winter.

3   *Thar She Blows*, by Captain John A. Cook, published by Chapman and Grimes, p. 76.

4   "The Story of Viola Cook," By Josef Berger (Jeremiahh Digges,) from *Cape Cod Pilot*, as printed in *The Cape Itself*, edited by Robert Finch, p. 118

5   *Thar She Blows*, p. 258.

6   Interestingly, when the *Bowhead* reached San Francisco, the crew sued Captain Cook for cruelty and they were able to recover damages – one of the few instances in the disposition of a maritime case where the ruling did not favor the ship's master in matters of discipline.

7   *Time and the Town: A Provincetown Chronicle*, by Mary Heaton Vorse, published by the Dial Press, New York, N.Y., 1942, p. 223.

Chapter 9. Didama Kelley Doane of West Harwich

1   *The Cap'n's Wife*, by Albert Joseph George, Syracuse University Press, Syracuse, New York, 1946, p. 43.

2   George, p. 60.

3   Brewster Historical Society archives. Mary was the wife of Captain Elijah E. Knowles. Descriptions of the difficult Cape Horn passage are a common feature in most journals. Thankful Chase Phillips wrote to her mother in Harwichport telling of an experience aboard her husband's barkentine *Laura R. Burnham* in November of 1879. "...we had nothing but bad weather for nearly four weeks. Gales of wind, rain, hail, and snow squalls. Headwinds all the time for five days. We sailed all the time and the fifth day was just where we started from. Had not gained one mile."

4   George, p. 66.

5   George, p. 69.

6   Ethelinda Lewis and her husband Valentine later had to abandon the *Corinthian* when the ship struck on Blossom Shoals about a year later. They had to spend almost twenty-four hours in an open boat among large ice floes before they were rescued.

7   George, p. 74.

8   George, p. 82.

9   George, p. 87.

10 In March of 1872, *Rival*, with another captain in charge, left Rangoon, Burma, bound for Falmouth, England. The ship never reached port and was presumed lost with all hands.

Chapter 10. Bethia Knowles Mayo Sears of Brewster

1   American Clipper Ships 1833-1858: Volume II, by Octavius T. Howe and Frederick C. Matthews, Dover Publications, Inc., New York, N.Y., 1986 edition, p. 707-709.

2   Journal entry, *Wild Ranger*, October 27, 1855. There is indication that Bethia was a plump young lady and the heat, with her extra weight, increased her discomfort.

3   Journal entry, Saturday, *Wild Ranger*, November 10, 1855.

4   Journal entry, Friday, *Wild Ranger*, November 22, 1855.

5   Journal entry, *Wild Ranger*, December 4, 1855.

6   Journal entry, *Wild Ranger*, December 29, 1855.

7   Journal entry, *Wild Ranger*, February 15, 1856.

8   Journal entry, *Wild Ranger*, March 17, 1856.

9   Journal entry, *Wild Ranger*, May 11, 1856.

10 Bethia's journal mentions a number of Cape Cod captains in Calcutta during her time there. These include Captain Thomas P. Howes and Captain Carleton Howes of Dennis, Captain Solomon Freeman Jr. and Elisha's uncle, Captain Freeman Bangs of Brewster.

11 Journal entry, *Wild Ranger*, June 27, 1856.

12 Journal entry, *Wild Ranger*, September 16, 1856.

13 Papers of Elisha F. Sears, *Wild Ranger*, Phillips Library, Salem, MA.

Chapter 11. Clara Freeman of Brewster

1   A transcript of Clara Freeman's journal is in the Brewster archives. The original is in the custody of the Brewster Ladies Library. All quotes are from the transcribed copy.

2   This large home was completed in 1860 and is presently being operated as an inn on Breakwater Road in Brewster, MA.

3   Some of these games would have included familiar children's activities like jacks, dominoes, and jackstraws – similar to modern "pick up sticks." Board games such as checkers were popular and if there was a playmate available, games of tag and races were played. Girls were encouraged to become skilled n a game called "graces" where a hoop would be tossed between partners with a pain a game called "graces" where a hoop would be tossed between partners with a pair of wooden rods, the intention being to encourage delicate movement and coordination.

4   This would have been her brother Willard, who was sixteen years older than Clara.

Chapter 12. Sarah Priscilla Weekes of Harwich

1   A younger daughter, Letella Linwood Weekes, then just two years old, was left with Captain Weekes' sister in Falmouth.

2   There is some question as to whether this was to be the baby's permanent name. The Weekes' genealogy does not list the child's name, noting that an unnamed child born to Darius and Rhoda Weekes "died soon." The short biography of Captain Weekes in Deyo's *History of Barnstable County* lists the child's name as Rosetta.

3   Scotland, 1966, p. 5.

4   Because of weight restrictions on cargo aboard the *Delaware*, the family was forced to ship the bulk of their valuables that had been collected during the two-year voyage aboard another vessel. That ship was lost off Georges Banks several weeks after their arrival home, taking to the bottom all of their treasures.

Chapter 13. Sally Mayo Dyer Lavender of Provincetown

1   In some references, Sally is also referred to as Sarah.

Notes 197

Unpublished Journals, Diaries, Letters and Rewminiscences Written by Seafaring Women

Addy, Persis Crowell. (Mrs. John). Transcribed letter of January 28, 1967, used through the courtesy of David and Nancy Sears of East Dennis, Massachusetts.

Coleman, Edith Nickerson. (Mrs. Bennett). Personal papers used through the courtesy of her grandson, Robert Coleman of Orleans, Massachusetts.

Freeman, Clara. Transcript of original diary from the Brewster Historical Archives. A serialized series of her letters to Rosalind Amelia Young, granddaughter of Edward Young, one of the original *H.M.S. Bounty* mutineers, is in the *Cape Cod Standard Times* newspaper, August 18, 1936.

Howes, Rebecca Wood. (Mrs. Barnabas). Diary of Rebecca Wood Howes 1875-1880. Transcription of the original diary by Peter Hemenway Baxter and Anne Hall Baxter. December 1972. Original diary is in the possession of the Baxter family.

Lavender, Sally Mayo. (Mrs. Joseph). Transcript of original 1854 sea journal from the Pilgrim Monument Museum, Provincetown, Massachusetts.

Park, Sylvia Snow Taylor. (Mrs. Jeremiah). Letters are part of the Park collection in the Harwich Historical Society. The majority of the collection contains letters from Captain Park to people at home on Cape Cod.

Phillips, Thankful Chase. (Mrs. Samuel). A single letter written in November of 18879 expressing concerns about the severity of the Cape Horn passage. Harwich Historical Society archives.

Ryder, Clara Cook. (Mrs. Stephen). Sea journal kept on board the whaler *N.D. Chase*, 1857-58. Transcribed copy at Pilgrim Monument Museum, Provincetown, Massachusetts.

Sears, Bethia Knowles Mayo. (Mrs. Elisha). Sea journal kept on clipper *Wild Ranger*, 1855-56. Log 656 1855-56W, Phillips Library, Peabody Essex Museum, Salem, Massachusetts.

Bibliography, Published Books and Articles

Baird, Donal. *Women at Sea in the Age of Sail*. Halifax, Nova Scotia: Nimbus Publishing Limited, 2001.

Baker, Florence K. *Yesterday's Tide*. South Yarmouth, MA: n.p., 1941.

Balano, James W., ed. *The Log of the Skipper's Wife*. Camden, ME: Down East Books, 1979.

Bockstoce, John R. *Whales, Ice, and Men: The History of Whaling in the Western Arctic*. Seattle, WA: University of Washington Press, 1986.

Boyce, Bertha Hamblin. *Bertha Goes Whaling*. Falmouth, MA: Kendall Printing Co., 1963.

Bray, Mary Matthews. *A Sea Trip in Clipper Ship Days*. Richard G. Badger, ed. Boston, MA: The Gorham Press, 1920.

Cabral, Reginald W. and James Theriault. *Wooden Ships and Iron Men*. Provincetown, MA: Trustees of the Heritage Museum, 1994.

Chapelle, Howard I. *The History of American Sailing Ships*. New York, NY: W.W. Norton, 1935.

Cook, John Atkins. *Pursuing the Whale*. Boston, MA: Houghton Mifflin Co., 1926.

_____. *Thar She Blows: Chasing Whales in the Arctic*. Boston, MA: Chapman and Grimes, 1937.

Cordingly, David. *Women Sailors & Sailors' Women: An Untold Maritime History*. New York, NY: Random House, 2001.

Creighton, Margaret S, and Lisa Nortling. eds. *Iron Men, Wooden Women, Gender and Seafaring in the Atlantic World, 1700-1920*. Baltimore MD: 1996.

Cutler, Carl. *Greyhounds of the Sea*. Annapolis, MD: Naval Institute Press, 1961.

De Pauw, Linda Grant. *Seafaring Women*. Boston, MA: Houghton Mifflin Co., 1982.

Deyo, Simeon L. *History of Barnstable County, Massachusetts*. New York, NY: H.W. Blake & Co., 1890.

Diddel, Margarita Thompson. *Thistle in Her Hand*. Interlaken, NY: Windswept Press, 1988.

Druett, Joan. *Petticoat Whalers: Whaling Wives at Sea, 1820-1920*. Auckland, NZ: Collins, 1991.

_____. *Hen Frigates: Passion and Peril, Nineteenth Century Women at Sea*. New York, , NY: Touchstone, 1998.

_____. "Those Female Journals." *The Log of Mystic Seaport* 40 (Winter 1988:) 115-24.

Fairburn, William Armstrong. *Merchant Sail*. Center Lovell, ME: Six volumes. Fairburn Marine Educational Foundation, Inc., 1947.

Ferguson, Georgia Knowles (Cook.) *And God Created Great Whales*. n.p.: 1976.

George, Albert Joseph. *The Cap'n's Wife*. Syracuse, NY: Syracuse University Press, 1946.

Hassell, Martha. *The Challenge of Hannah Rebecca*. Sandwich, MA: Sandwich Historical Society, 1986.

Hegarty, Reginald B. *Returns of Whaling Vessels Sailing From American Ports: A Continuation of Alexander Starbuck's "History of the American Whale Fishery"* 1878-1928. New Bedford, MA: Old Dartmouth Historical Society and Whaling Museum, 1959.

Hoyt, Henry Sears Jr., and Ann Hoyt Stone. *Looking Aft: A Personal History of the Family of Captain J. Henry Sears of Brewster, Massachusetts in the Clipper Ship Era*. Lunenberg, VT: Stinehour Press, 1997.

Howe, Octavius T., and Frederick C. Matthews. *American Clipper Ships 1833-1858*. Volumes I & II. Mineola, NY: Dover Publishing, 1986.

Keene, Betsy D. *History of Bourne: From 1622-1937*. Yarmouthport, MA: Charles W. Swift, Publishing, 1937.

Kilian, Bernard. *The Voyage of the Schooner Polar Bear: Whaling and Trading in the North Pacific and Arctic, 1913-1914*. John Bockstoce, ed. New Bedford, MA: Published by the Old Dartmouth Historical Society and the Alaska Historical Commission, 1983.

Kitterege, Henry C. *Shipmasters of Cape Cod*. Boston, MA: Houghton Mifflin Co., 1935.

Lawrence, Mary Chipman. *The Captain's Best Mate: The Journal of Mary Chipman Lawrence on the Whaler "Addison," 1856-1860*. Edited and with introduction and appendices by Stanton Garner Providence, RI: Brown University Press, 1966.

Lubbock, Basil. *The Nitrate Clippers*. Glasgow, Scotland: Brown, Son & Ferguson, Ltd., 1966.

Lund, Judith Navas. *Whaling Masters and Whaling Voyages Sailing from American Ports: A Compilation of Sources*. New Bedford, MA: New Bedford Whaling Museum, Kendall Whaling Museum, Ten Pound Island Book Co., 2001.

Malloy, Mary. *Whaling Brides and Whaling Brothers: The Lawrences of Falmouth*. Falmouth, MA: Falmouth Historical Society, 1997.

Matthews, Frederick C. *American Merchant Ships 1850-1900*. Two Volumes. New York, NY: Dover Publications Inc., 1987.

Morison, Samuel Eliot. *Maritime History of Massachusetts 1783-1860*. Boston, MA: Houghton Mifflin Co., 1921.

Paine, Mildred B. et al. *Harwich Men of the Sea*. Harwich, MA: Harwich Historical Commission, 1977.

Reid, Nancy Thacher. *Dennis, Cape Cod: From First Comers to Newcomers 1639-1993*. Dennis, MA: Dennis Historical Society, 1996.

Rex, Persy Felitz. *The Prolific Pencil*. Fredrika A. Burrows ed. Taunton, MA: William S. Sullwold Publishing, Inc., 1980.

Robotti, Frances Diane. *Whaling and Old Salem (A Chronicle of the Sea)*. New York, NY: Bonanza Books, 1962.

Ryder, Marion Crowell. *Cape Cod Remembrances*. Taunton, MA: William S. Sullwold Publishing, Inc., 1972.

Sears, J. Henry. *Brewster Ship Masters*. Yarmouthport, MA: G.W. Swift, 1906.

Shaw, David W. *Flying Cloud: The True Story of America's Most Famous Clipper Ship and the Woman Who Guided Her*. New York NY: William Morrow, 2000.

Shay, Edith and Frank. *Sand in Their Shoes: A Cape Cod Reader*. Boston, MA: Houghton Mifflin Co., 1951.

Sherman, Stuart C. Judith M. Downey and Virginia M. Adams, eds. *Whaling Logbooks and Journals 1613-1928: An Inventory of Manuscript Records in Public Collections*. New York, NY: Garland Publishing, 1986.

Sprague, Francis William. *Barnstable and Yarmouth Sea Captains and Shipowners*. Brookline, MA: n.p., 1913.

Springer, Haskell. "The Captain's Wife at Sea." In *Iron Men, Wooden Women: Gender and Seafaring in the Atlantic World, 1700-1920*. Margaret S. Creighton and Lisa Norling, eds. Baltimore, MD: Johns Hopkins University Press, 1996. Pp. 92-117.

Stark, Suzanne J. *Female Tars: Women Aboard Ship in the Age of Sail*. Annapolis, MD: Naval Institute Press, 1996.

Swift, Theodore W., "Yarmouth Shipmasters." *The Yarmouth Register*. Yarmouthport, MA: August 17, 1935.

_____. "Yarmouth Shipmasters." *The Yarmouth Register*. Yarmouthport, MA: February 16, 1935.

Trayser, Donald. *Barnstable: Three Centuries of a Cape Cod Town*. Hyannis, MA: F.B. & F.P. Goss, 1939.

Vorse, Mary Heaton. *Time and the Town: A Provincetown Chronicle*. New York, NY: The Dial Press, 1942.

Ward, R. Gerard, ed. *American Activities in the Central Pacific 1790-1870/* Volumes 1-8. Ridgewood, NJ: The Gregg Press, 1967.

Weekes, Sarah Priscilla (Foster.) *Two Years on Shipboard*. Newport, VT: Bullock Press, 1916.

Whiting, Emma Mayhew and Henry Beetle Hough. *Whaling Wives*. Boston, MA: Houghton Mifflin Co., 1953.

Wood, Tim. "Letter Details Tragic Loss of a Child at Sea in 1856." Chatham, MA: In *The Cape Cod Chronicle*, July 20, 1995.

Jim Coogan in front of the Sturgis Library, Barnstable, Massachusetts. Photograph by Elizabeth Friend.

About the Author

Jim Coogan was raised on Cape Cod and grew up in Brewster. Now retired after almost three decades as a high school history teacher, he has written thirteen books about the Cape, five of them with his writing partner, Jack Sheedy. A former long-time *Cape Cod Times* columnist, Jim is a popular lecturer on topics related to Cape Cod and its history and is a frequent contributor to area magazines and newspapers. Jim's first novel, *Sears Point*, was published in 2016. A second novel, *Cape Cod Passage*, was released in 2022. Both books are available on Amazon. Jim lives in Sandwich, Massachusetts.

Made in the USA
Middletown, DE
27 May 2024

54798232R00117